IN THE FOOTSTEPS OF SAINT AUGUSTINE

THE GREAT ENGLISH PILGRIMAGE

FROM ROME TO CANTERBURY

BY THE SAME AUTHOR

A Guide to St Martin's Church, Canterbury. 1966

Stour Valley Walks in illustrated folders (3). Stour Valley Society. 1974, 1979, 1982

Save the Stour, and other poems illustrated by John Ward RA. Stour Valley Press. 1974 (Revised 1990)

A Manual for those prepared to give TIME to Pray. 1975 (Revised 1981)

The Magic Paperboat Treasurehunt: a story for young children by Grandpa Crookes. Carousel. 1979.

Martin of Tours – A Study of parish life of Christians in the 4th century. Routledge and Kegan Paul. 1980

Martinus Van Tours: een biografie. Gooi & Sticht. 1980

Six Walks along the Stour from Canterbury to Sandwich. Meresborough Books. 1985

Rising from the Root: the early Christians and tomorrow's Church. Beaminster Area Team Publication. 1985

The New Springtime of the Church a prophecy. The Canterbury Press Norwich. 1992

IN THE FOOTSTEPS OF
SAINT AUGUSTINE

The Great English Pilgrimage

FROM ROME TO CANTERBURY

1400th Anniversary AD 597–1997

CHRISTOPHER DONALDSON

Foreword by

DAVID SAY KCVO

The Canterbury Press
Norwich

© Christopher Donaldson 1995

First published 1995 by The Canterbury Press Norwich
(a publishing imprint of Hymns Ancient & Modern Limited,
a registered charity)
St Mary's Works, St Mary's Plain,
Norwich, Norfolk, NR3 3BN

British Library Cataloguing in Publication Data

A catalogue record for this book is available
from the British Library

ISBN 1–85311–064–7 (Hardback)
ISBN 1–85311–098–1 (Paperback)

Typeset by Datix International Limited, Bungay, Suffolk
and Printed and bound in Great Britain
by Bell and Bain Ltd, Glasgow

DEDICATED

TO ALL PILGRIMS

ON THE WAY

FOREWORD

BY THE RIGHT REVD DR R. D. SAY, KCVO
Assistant Bishop in the diocese of Canterbury

IN 1997 the fourteen hundredth anniversary of St Augustine's pilgrimage from Rome to Canterbury will be commemorated in the City of Canterbury, in the ancient Abbey which bears his name and in the Cathedral of which for seven short but exciting years he was the first bishop. A national pilgrimage will include groups from various parts of the British Isles and pilgrims are also expected from Rome and other European centres. These celebrations will be greatly enhanced by Christopher Donaldson's account of his own pilgrimage from Rome to Canterbury in the steps of St Augustine. He was no energetic 'back packer' or comfortable motorist, but one who used public transport throughout his recent journey.

This book is before all else a personal diary of a demanding adventure which, albeit as a 'senior citizen', the author clearly enjoyed to the full. But it also includes informed extracts from a historian's notebook that enliven both the account of St Augustine's mission with his forty companions and also that of Mr Donaldson's pilgrimage as a lone traveller following in Augustine's footsteps.

As a former Vicar of St Martin's Church in Canterbury, the oldest parish church in England built in Roman times and still in use for regular worship today, Christopher Donaldson is careful to acknowledge that St Augustine was sent by Pope Gregory to a country where Christianity had already taken root. Augustine's task was to bring fresh missionary zeal and an ordered structure to the Church in England, in the same way as Lanfranc, Anselm and their fellow Benedictines, from Bec in Normandy, were called upon to do six centuries later.

The relationship of Church and state is today a matter of topical debate. All who follow in the steps of St Augustine from Rome to Canterbury will be helped to a fresh understanding of the deep roots of the historic relationship of Church and Crown. They will also realize why it is that Anglicans throughout the world, by no means all of them English speaking, look to Canterbury as their Mother Church and to the Archbishop of Canterbury, both as Augustine's 102nd successor and as first among equals in the leadership of the Anglican Communion in the world of today.

+ DAVID SAY

Give me my scallop-shell of quiet,
My staff of faith to walk upon,
My scrip of joy, immortal diet,
My bottle of salvation,
My gown of glory, hope's true gage,
And thus I'll take my pilgrimage.'

Sir Walter Ralegh.

The shell is the pilgrimage logo
of the Council of Churches for Britain and Ireland

Saint Augustine, after window in North-West Transept, Canterbury Cathedral

Preface

THE IDEA of this Pilgrimage came from four clear Canterbury hunches, urges, or prophecies, beginning in my childhood days. In a strange way all in turn have worked out and fused together into this Pilgrimage so that like Paul, I was determined to go to Rome. I planned to go to see Rome for myself; to stand there at the Church of San Gregorio Magno, where the then Archbishop of Canterbury, Robert Runcie, celebrated Vespers in October 1990 with Pope John Paul II, because that marks the precise spot where Augustine was commissioned by Gregory the Great to go to England in AD 596 to take Christianity to the English people. Now in 1997 we celebrate the fourteen hundredth anniversary of St Augustine coming to Canterbury, and I hope many pilgrims will find this book a helpful guide.

CHRISTOPHER DONALDSON

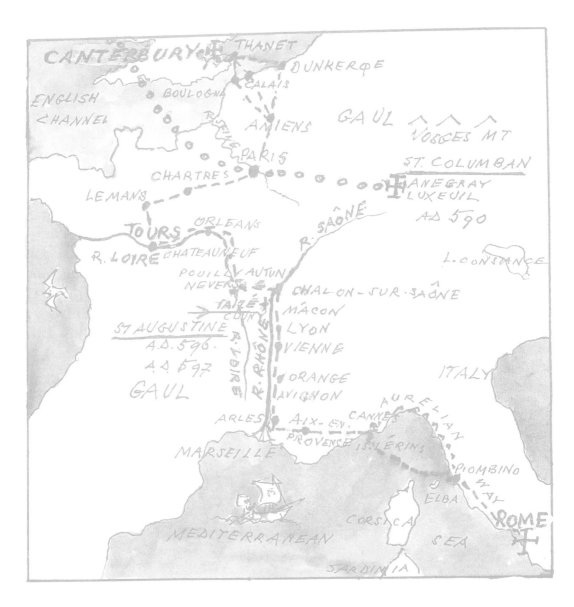

597 – THE PILGRIMAGE ROUTE – 1997

Contents

ACKNOWLEDGEMENTS

I AM indebted to all those who have helped me
in this exciting task. To John and Diana Morgan
of Hinton who egged me on from the beginning.
To Barbara Wrigley of Merriott who gave much
advice on Rome. To Douglas Brown and Ralph
Martin, S.S.M. who gave me such a helpful week
at the Anglican Centre in Rome. To John Heaton,
Gwen Blum and my agent Mary Harding for all
their work typing and editing. To Penguin
Classics, *The History of the Franks* by Gregory of
Tours (translated by Lewis Thorpe) 1974; and
Veritas, *Columbanus in his own words* by Tomas O
Fiaich, for permission to quote from their books, to
Routledge and Kegan Paul for permission to
reproduce three drawings (pp. 25, 36, 153) from the
author's earlier book *Martin of Tours*, also to
Kenneth Baker, the Project Development Manager of
The Canterbury Press Norwich, Norfolk, for his
unfailing encouragement throughout the production
of this book.

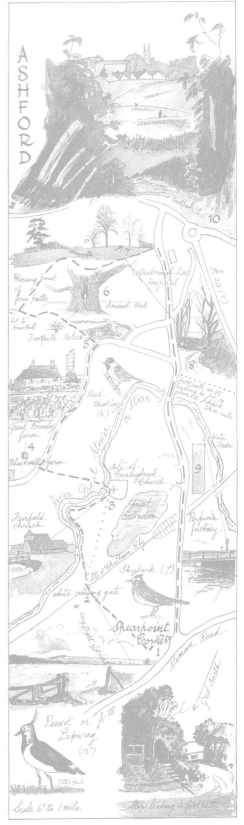

From Walks in the Stour Valley: No. 6

Introduction

My first hunch – the Great Stour Valley, Kent

At the age of twelve I went to the King's School at Canterbury, just in the shadow of the great and awesome Cathedral. But it was the clear waters of the river Great Stour as it flows through its meadows and under the city that I first loved with a passion. I spent many hours bathing in it and rowing or sailing on it, and out of a childish urge I made a prophecy, or had a hunch, that one day I would explore the river to its source, and then sail down through Canterbury to the open sea. It took me sixty years before I fulfilled that prophecy, as only then did I start to chart the statutory footpaths on the ordnance survey maps, up and down the valley to where the stream gushes out of the hillside at Lenham near Maidstone. As I went I made maps, illustrated them and wrote notes of the walks.

I developed a number of these maps which were sold in folders to help others to follow these paths. I walked and sailed many time from Canterbury to the open sea and St Augustine's Cross at Ebbsfleet on the Island of Thanet. At last I wrote a book on it all with maps and illustrations which was published under the title *Six Walks along the Stour from Canterbury to Sandwich*. Only as recently as 1990 when I was asked to cut the ribbon to open the Stour Valley Walk, which had by then been developed by Kent County Council to become one of England's Long Distance Footpaths, was I able to feel my first hunch or prophecy had been fulfilled. But then, this river which has haunted me for so long had surprises yet in store.

My second hunch – the influence of St Martin

When I was forty five, Archbishop Michael Ramsey invited me to become Rector of England's oldest parish church, St Martin's, outside the city walls of Canterbury. The Venerable Bede who lived at Jarrow and died in AD 735 wrote of it: 'There was on the East side of the city, a Church dedicated to the honour of St Martin, built whilst the Romans were still in the island, wherein the queen [Bertha], who was a Christian used to pray. In this, Augustine and his companions first began to meet, to sing, to pray, to say mass, to preach and to baptize . . .' As I celebrated the Eucharist and preached, or baptized, married or buried these very English people I always delighted that I was standing on the spot where Augustine had arrived in AD 597 after Pope Gregory had sent him from San Gregorio Magno in Rome. It sent thrills through my veins. For ten years with all the outbursts of joy over the ecumenical events of the Second Vatican Council going on all around me, I used to sit there quietly waiting on God to speak to me, until slowly there came my second hunch or prophecy. The strange Roman stones started to speak to me as T. S. Eliot wrote in his *Four Quartets*: 'What the dead had no speech for when living, they can tell you, being dead'.

I was thrilled to be there. I snatched time in my busy life to research St Martin and wrote a guide book for St Martin's church, which has since gone into many editions. Out of my research I came face to face with that strange uncouth monk Martin, almost as if he were alive. I found three weighty books about him in St Augustine's Library, written by his young friend and companion Sulpitius Severus (AD 363–420) and the story he

told was a total revelation for me. I was transported by Martin and Sulpitius into the clear air of the century of the Nicene Creed (AD 325), where the very word 'ecumenical' had its Christian origins. As I sat in St Martin's I realised that the very stones of this church in which Augustine and his companions and the English people had come to terms with Christianity some fourteen hundred years ago were far older than that. While the Romans with their legions still lived in Britain, this building as early as the fourth century AD, had heard the sounds of some unknown group of converted Christians keeping eucharist together and warming to the enthusiasm of Martin and his missions.

In the year 1975 the Archbishop gave me a six months sabbatical to try to write a book on Martin. For two months I stayed at the Benedictine Abbey at Ligugé, near Poitiers, where Martin had spent the ten happiest years of his life, living on the site of a ruined villa given to him by Hilary, Bishop of Poitiers. I

St Martin's Church, Stour Valley and the Cathedral

had the freedom of the library and it was my joy to receive each day the Eucharist with the Roman Catholic brothers at their concelebration, for which the Bishop had given me permission. Later I went on to stay with the sisters at Marmoutier, near Tours, by the caves where Martin's cell is. Finally I walked many miles to make pilgrimage to Candes, where Martin died in AD 397. To my surprise I found that Pope John XXIII, who later called together the Second Vatican Council, had made the same pilgrimage to this lovely place before me, because of his special devotion to Martin.

Back home I finished my sabbatical by making a most exciting journey by motorcycle, following up all the Martin places associated with the Roman occupation of Britain, and this led me in the end to the island of Whithorn in Scotland, to find St Ninian's Cave, the same Ninian who is reputed to have met Martin at Marmoutier. I now realise that Martin for me was indeed a gold mine. As this pilgrimage develops it will become clear how, not only was he the Apostle of Gaul (France and West Germany), but that it was he who directly opened the doors for the English people to accept Christianity. Martin's name appears as church dedications in so many villages and towns throughout Europe and England that one can see how his strange fame and his continuing influence in intercession after his death was instrumental in ushering in the Middle Ages. For example, a letter of Sulpitius left a most powerful influence on millions of people for centuries, and still does: 'Martin, poor and insignificant on earth, has a rich entrance granted him into heaven. From that blessed region, as I trust, he looks upon me as my guardian, while I am writing these things, and upon you while you read them'. My empathy with Martin was complete.

My third hunch – a vision for the reshaping of the churches in the nineties.

Back in Canterbury after my sabbatical leave I was so restless I had to move. My wife and I found a cottage in the Dorset hills in a hamlet near Racedown (where William and Dorothy Wordsworth stayed and wrote, and were joined by Samuel Coleridge). It was here that I wrote my book *Martin of Tours*.

Out of the quiet and homeliness of the countryside and looking down each morning on the Axe valley below, I lived, in a way, like a solitary or hermit with my wife and family. Full of the vision of Martin and the early Christian ecumenical communities of the first four centuries, I had the chance is an unhurried way, to make meditations and to read the morning and evening prayers of the church quietly.

Then slowly again, out of the silences in waiting on God to speak to me, came the third hunch or prophecy that could not be gainsaid, and which had brought me so much frustration and upheaval. My studies into St Martin had led me into a knowledge of the parish system of the early Christian Church and its much simpler style of Christianity. I had learnt from him, from Ambrose and from Cyprian of a Church holy catholic and apostolic indeed, yet quite uncluttered by administration or denominations which over the years have developed. As I knew only too well 'there was never anything by the wit of man so well devised, or so sure established which in continuance of time hath not been corrupted' (Book of Common Prayer). I could at the same time see how many of our bishops, clergy and laity, with courage and insights, were beginning to sense the emerging of a new springtime of the Church and I longed to enunciate it with all its hopefulness. I poured out my vision of how it had all come to me out of the hard won experience of thirty years as a parish priest and out of my love for the early Christian church that I was discovering. When I had finished the typescript I walked over the valley to the small church of Wayford with its thatched roof, and laid it on the altar and prayed to God to bless its prophecy. The typescript had many rejections from publishers, but in 1985 the Beaminster Team of parishes in Dorset determined to publish a part of the book as a paperback. This was called *Rising from the Root – the early Christians and tomorrow's Church*. It sold well and I have since developed the theme into a further book *The New Spring-time of the Church*, which presents a prophecy of how the Churches in England are beginning to shape under the ecumenical climate of the nineties. A third prophecy had at last been enunciated.

My fourth hunch – in the footsteps of St Augustine

From these three hunches I go back to the first, the river Great Stour, for my fourth prophecy. 'I must go on to see Rome as well'. Here I was, within me still that child in his boat in the enchanted world of the river Stour, and behind me all those booklets, folders and articles written, endless talks given and even a

society founded. My next plan was to write a small booklet to guide pilgrims on their way from St Augustine's Cross at Ebbsfleet to Canterbury, but then I received a letter from Mr Nigel Nicolson, the author of *Sissinghurst Castle* (also a lover of the Stour). He wrote: 'You might extend the story about St Augustine's mission from where it began, at St Andrew's Monastery on the Caelian Hill, where last year I saw a tablet commemorating the event . . .'; it was for me like Beauty and the Beast, when the doors opened of their own accord, inviting me to go into the castle. The hunch quickly developed with all its excitement, and its absorbing research has broadened into the journey of a lifetime, for others to follow and work on for many years to come.

For me this pilgrimage is a spiritual exercise. For others, too, of all denominations or none, to go together, not as strangers but as pilgrims, will make a dent in Satan's armour and help to spark off what we are all learning to call the Inter church Process, the new emerging way towards unity. The pilgrimage will eventually become a vivid part of the Decade of Evangelism in Britain. In May 1997 at Ebbsfleet on the Isle of Thanet there will be celebrations to mark St Augustine's landing there in AD 597, fourteen hundred years ago. In that same year the sixteen hundredth anniversary of St Martin's death in AD 397 falling on 11 November will fill many with thoughts of Martin's mission to Gaul and Britain and perhaps remind us to re-establish him as the long-forgotten saint of our Modern Remembrance Day. As a Roman legionary he had fought an important battle at Worms in AD 356 without bloodshed, and won a free armistice. For after the signing of the armistice of 1918, on the eleventh hour of the eleventh day of the eleventh month, Marshal Ferdinand Foch went to the tomb at the Basilica of St Martin at Tours to lead a great *Te Deum* of thanksgiving that all the years of bloodshed and hostilities had ended.

My Pilgrimage Plans

I planned to spend a week or so in Rome, and once there I hoped to see for myself some of the catacombs where the early Christians kept eucharist in those terrifying days of the persecutions long ago. I hoped to trace the sights sacred to Gregory's and Augustine's presence there; to keep vigil by the tablet at San Gregorio al Celio and then to ask one of the Benedictine community to give me a missionary benediction before setting off for Canterbury. I planned to travel by train and ferry, following Augustine's route over the sea to Nice and Lérins, then up the Rhône and Sâone and down the Loire; on to Tours, then to Chartres, Paris and Dunquerque. I would cross the Channel by ferry and see St Augustine's Cross at Ebbsfleet on the Island of Thanet, that I know so well, standing there to welcome me home to England. Finally I planned to walk or sail up the river Great Stour to Canterbury. I planned to fulfil my longing to pray quietly as I went. I felt all those sacred places would speak to me of a truly ecumenical pilgrimage full of the spirituality such as we are being taught by Mother Teresa and the Brothers at Taizé. I planned to write up my diary every day and illustrate it with drawings and photographs as a sort of pathfinder pilgrimage for those who come after me.

As you will discover, not everything went according to plan, but I am thrilled that The Canterbury Press Norwich has agreed to publish the outcome and make it available in this illustrated book.

St Augustine's Cross, near Ebbsfleet, in Thanet

CHRONOLOGICAL TABLE

Date	Character	Event
AD		
304	DIOCLETIAN, EMPEROR	The height of the persecution of Christians.
306	CONSTANTINE, EMPEROR	Acclaimed as Augustus by the troops at York.
312		Wins the battle of the Milvian Bridge, and sees the vision of the cross in the sky.
313		Edict of Milan and toleration of Christianity.
316	ST MARTIN	Born at Sabaria in Pannonia.
371		Elected Bishop of Tours against his will.
397		Dies at Candes on 11 November; his body is taken to Tours and a church is built for him, and miracles begin.
407		River Rhine freezes over. The barbarians pour across the Roman frontiers, among them the Salian Franks, who by conquest, often defeat the Legions. The Christians survive the onslaught, and often influence the pagans.
450	KINGS HENGIST and HORSA	The Jutes land in Kent and gradually expel the Britons from the area.
460	CLOVIS	Born, and becomes in . . .
493		King of the Franks. Marries the Burgundian princess, CLOTILD.
496		He is Baptized as a Christian at Rheims,
508		At Tours, in St Martin's Church he take to himself the consulship as Emperor.
511		Calls a Church Council at Orleans. Dies.
539	BISHOP GREGORY OF TOURS	Born at Clermont-Ferrand.
540	POPE GREGORY THE GREAT	Born at Rome.
543	ST COLUMBAN	Born at Leinster in Ireland
544	QUEEN CLOTILD	Dies at Tours and buried at St Genevieve in Paris.
560	KING ETHELBERT	Crowned King of Kent
561	KING LOTHAR I	Goes on Pilgrimage to St Martin's Church at Tours. Dies. His four sons divide the kingdom between themselves, and Charibert becomes King of Paris.
561	KING CHARIBERT	Marries QUEEN INGOBERG, and she gives birth to a daughter, the PRINCESS BERTHA. The Queen retires to live with Bertha in religious seclusion at Le Mans.
567		King Charibert, dies, having arranged for Bertha to have her marriage solemnised by Christian rites.
573	GREGORY OF TOURS	Consecrated Bishop of Tours.

578   ST GREGORY THE GREAT   Ordained as the seventh deacon of Rome. Sent as resident ambassador in the imperial court at Constantinople.

586   Returns to Rome as abbot of St Andrew's.

590   3 September, consecrated Bishop of Rome and Pope.

593   ST COLUMBAN   He with his group land in Gaul, and eventually settle at Luxeuil in the Haute-Saône.

594   GREGORY OF TOURS   Dies.

596   ST GREGORY THE GREAT   Appoints Augustine and forty companions to set out to convert the English people to Christianity.

597   QUEEN FREDEGUND   Dies, and QUEEN BRUNHILDA assists the mission and rebukes Columban.

597   ST AUGUSTINE   Lands with his companions in Thanet and is made welcome by KING ETHELBERT and QUEEN BERTHA. They are invited to worship in ST MARTIN'S and the mission begins in earnest in Canterbury.

Bede from a window in Norwich Cathedral

CHAPTER ONE

Characters to Meet on the Pilgrimage

HERE are some of the characters who made the first great English Christian pilgrimage with Augustine from Rome to Canterbury in AD 596–597, or who helped to arrange it all or who by their accounts bring them alive for us today. Among the fascinating characters to meet are: the Venerable Bede, the scholar, who, though full of Rome never made it there himself; Pope Gregory of Rome, who dominates the whole scene of the pilgrimage from one end to the other, though he never entered Canterbury; Bishop Gregory of Tours who in his ten great books gives perhaps the most vivid accounts (often verbatim) of what life was like in Gaul at the time, though he himself never went to Rome.

Other characters are the 'dirty' Lombards, with their delightful Queen Theodelinda; the handsome and haughty Dowager Queen Brunhilda of Gaul, who gave such powerful protection to the pilgrims on their way to Canterbury, and yet came to such a cruel death; Ethelbert the Saxon king and his quiet saintly queen Bertha, and her mother Ingoberg of Tours; the wild Irish Columban with his freelance twelve companions walking straight across Augustine's footpath to settle at Luxeuil; and above all the strange supernatural power of the long dead Saint Martin, who broods over the whole scene from Tours, at Gaul and the British Isles and seems to guide and protect the caravans of pilgrims on their ways. All these characters, and many even more startling, make the journey most exciting for the modern pilgrimage treading in their footsteps.

The Venerable Bede

The Venerable Bede (AD 673–735) sets the scene in his Ecclesiastical History. Bede was born near the Benedictine monastery of Jarrow near South Shields, and at the age of seven was sent to the monastery school. He was from the beginning a natural scholar with a passion for learning. The quiet religious life absorbed him, the deep sonorous chant, the seven times a day psalmody, the solemn liturgy, the steady round of the seasons with the gardening and work on the farm. He learned to write with the quill pen. He loved the precise beauty of the calligraphy, and he mastered shorthand. He learnt Greek, Latin and Hebrew and helped to create the English language as it emerged from the language of the Anglo Saxons. When his religious duties were over and he was alone in his own beloved cell he could pour his heart into writing books and endless correspondence. To his joy he was made deacon at the age of nineteen and then priest when he was thirty. He began by writing commentaries and the lives of the saints; but then it seemed as if the Holy Spirit was driving him on towards a great undertaking and he settled down to his life's work the *Ecclesiastical History of the English People*, describing the development of his own peoples, from the time of the occupation of Britain by Julius Caesar in 54 BC to the death of the archbishop Bertwald in AD 731. His five large volumes consist of many chapters that cover some eight hundred years and he dwells on the conversion of the Anglo Saxon tribes to Christianity. Above all he gives a vivid description of Pope Gregory sending off Augustine and his companions from Rome, and their arrival at Ebbsfleet opposite Richborough castle on the island of Thanet.

Though Bede's account was written some one hundred and thirty years after the actual events in 597, yet he is no mere fanciful hagiographer, for his work is generally acknowledged by historians as having the very ring of truth in it all. As he himself wrote in his preface:

> My principal authority and aid in this work was the learned and reverend Abbot Albinus; who, educated in the Church of Canterbury by those venerable and learned men, Archbishop Theodore of blessed memory, and the Abbot Adrian, transmitted to me by Nothelm, the pious priest of the Church of London, either in writing or by word of mouth of the same Nothelm, all that he thought worthy of memory, that had been done in the province of Kent, or the adjacent parts, by the disciples of the blessed Pope Gregory, as he had learned the same either from writ-

ten records or the traditions of his ancestors.

Having established his credentials Bede later gives an account of St Augustine's arrival at Ebbsfleet and his journey to Canterbury. It will be our excitement to read this account and make our way along the old roman roads or river Great Stour as they did, until we arrive at St Martin's church in Canterbury, where Augustine, Queen Bertha and King Ethelbert worshipped: then to find the beginnings of the great cathedral, the roman ruins of St Pancras church and the great abbey ruins and tombs of the saints there.

Pope Gregory of Rome

Bede now introduces us to his real hero, Pope Gregory, 'the servant of the servants of God':

> Of whom, in regard that he by his zeal converted our nation, the English, from the power of Satan to the faith of Christ, it behoves us to discourse more at large in our Ecclesiastical History, for we may and ought rightly to call him our apostle, because, whereas he bore the pontifical power over all the world, and was placed over the churches already reduced to the faith of truth, he made our nation, till then given up to idols, the Church of Christ, so that we may be allowed to attribute to him the character of an apostle; for though he is not an apostle to others, yet he is so to us; we are the seal of his apostleship in our Lord.

Gregory was born in Rome about the year 540 of an old fashioned, Christian senatorial family who owned a villa on the Caelian Hill (the spot where our pilgrimage begins), and also owned many lucrative estates in Sicily. He entered his public career aged thirty-four, as a young prefect of the city, but after two or three-years, on his parents' death, sold his estates in Sicily, founded monasteries there, and gave his own palace on the Caelian Hill in Rome to become a monastery dedicated to St Andrew, whilst he joined as an ordinary monk.

Gregory was, however, no ordinary monk for he had vast personal drive and charisma which eventually drove him out into the world. His first battleground was with his own powerful sexual drive, which sometimes seemed as if it was the devil himself in him. The weapons he used against this devil were contemplation, the study of the scriptures and the liturgy, which at times seemed hardly enough to constrain him. Later, as Pope, he attacked the English people with a crude indelicacy which might even today offend. Bede describes Gregory's answers to poor Augustine's question 'whether after an illusion such as happens in a dream, any man may receive the body of our Lord, or if he is a priest, celebrate the divine mysteries?' Gregory's answer takes the form of a long discourse on the delicate nature of sexuality which comes as a dire warning: 'For all sin is fulfilled in three ways, viz., by suggestion, by delight and by consent. Suggestion is occasioned by the devil, delight is from the flesh, and consent from the mind.' This repressed sexual drive could make him edgy to the point of using physical violence in Jesus Christ's name; for example when one of Gregory's monks, called Justus, fell ill and sensed that he was going to die, he told a brother that he had secretly hidden three valuable golden coins and was now ashamed. When Gregory heard this he said that no one was

Pope Gregory, his father and mother: from a contemporary sketch by John the Deacon

to go near him or help him, and when he died his body was to be cast out on a dunghill with the three gold coins, and monks were to cry: To hell with you and your money.

In spite of this vicious crudeness some of the most intelligent, able and dynamic women of Gregory's generation were fascinated by him, and in a bloodthirsty world it was they and not the men who shaped the Christian culture of Europe. It was Gregory's letters to queen Bertha the Frank which opened up the mission for the conversion of the English; it was his letters to the powerful queen regent, Brunhilda, of the Frankish nation, which ensured safe conduct for Augustine's mission to travel from the Isle of Lérins near Nice to Thanet in Kent; and it was the encouragement of queen Theodelinda in her Lombard court near Milan which restrained her husband Agilulf and his lords from sacking Rome when they reached the gates of the city. All these powerful women were fascinated by Gregory's glamour and he in turn gladly exploited their infatuation.

Although he was such a spiritual giant, Gregory was a little man, as John the deacon describes him:

> . . . his beard of a rather tawny colour, rather bald, so that in the middle of his forehead he had two small neat curls, his darkish hair nicely curled and hanging down, his eyes had dark pupils, his nose thin and straight, slightly aquiline, his mouth was red, lips thick and subdivided, he had beautiful hands, with tapering fingers, well adapted for writing.

Gregory longed to be a humble monk and live the rigours of the common rule. He wanted to spend the still hours in contemplation and let Christ have his way with him, then to pour out his heart in writing, especially on the Scriptures.

But with his dynamic character he was not to be trapped in the cloister. The ageing pope, Pelagius II ordained Gregory under solemn duty, monk though he was, to be the seventh archdeacon of Rome, and to become resident ambassador at the imperial court in Constantinople. There he was to explain to the Emperor Maurice the shocking situation that was developing in Rome, with the violent Lombards rampaging through Italy on their way towards Rome itself, and with recurrent plagues infecting the city. Gregory served nine years in Constantinople and was then returned to Rome. There his community elected him as abbot of his own monastery, and he had the joy of four more years of undisturbed quiet

in which he completed his famous book on Job, and delivered lectures on the books of the Kings, the Prophets and the Song of Songs.

It was one day as he was passing through the Forum with his community that he had the prophetic hunch or vision that he wished to restore Christianity to Britain, and especially to the English people. Bede described the occasion:

> It is reported, that some merchants, having just arrived at Rome on a certain day, exposed many things for sale in the market-place, and abundance of people resorted thither to buy: Gregory himself went with the rest, and, among other things, some boys were set to sale, their bodies white, their countenances beautiful, and their hair very fine. Having viewed them he asked, as is said, from what country or nation they were brought? and was told, from the island of Britain, whose inhabitants were of such personal appearance. He again inquired whether those islanders were Christians, or still involved in the errors of paganism? and was informed that they were pagans. Then fetching a deep sigh from the bottom of his heart, 'Alas! What pity,' said he, 'that the author of darkness is possessed of men of such fair countenances and that being remarkable for such graceful aspects, their minds should be void of inward grace.' He therefore asked again, what was the name of that nation? and was answered, that they were called Angles. 'Right,' said he, 'for they have an Angelic face, and it becomes such to be co-heirs with the Angels in heaven.' 'What is the name,' proceeded he, 'of the province from which they are brought?' It was replied, that the natives of that province were called Deiri. 'Truly are they De ira,' said he, 'withdrawn from wrath, and called to the mercy of Christ. How is the king of that province called?' They told him his name was Aella; and he, alluding to the name, said, 'Hallelujah, the

praise of God the Creator must be sung in those parts'. (Bede, Book II.1)

Gregory then said to the Pope that out of his vision he would immediately send some ministers of the word into Britain, and that he would lead the group himself. The citizens of Rome would have none of it, knowing what a powerful leader he was. However, Gregory never forgot the vision. It lay buried in his mind, ready to come into play, like a flash at the right psychological moment.

Those four years of quietness in the monastery were suddenly shattered. In 590 the Tiber burst its banks; bubonic plague hit the city and many died through swellings in the groin. The first to die was Pope Pelagius II himself. The hated Lombards were on the march determined to sack Rome, and the people of Rome were thoroughly demoralised.

At such a time the only hope was that some charismatic saviour might appear to gather together the grieving Christian spirituality of so many and infuse some moral fibre into the people of Rome. Instinctively every eye turned to Gregory, their young Roman born prefect, now archdeacon and monk, where he was hiding in his own monastery. By public acclamation the people demanded that he should be made pope. He was horrified, and as Gregory of Tours wrote: 'he was preparing for flight and concealment, when he was seized and carried off and dragged to the basilica of St Peter'. Overwhelmed with what had happened, he soon recovered from the shock, and even before his enthronement he set immediately to work.

Out of the hours of contemplation, out of the fasts, out of the fight with self control and out of the daily psalmody grew clarity and determination. He knew exactly what to do in a practical way. The plague was a punishment from God, therefore Rome must do penance. A miracle was needed. He demanded that the clergy, monks and people should sing psalms uninterruptedly for three whole days. Seven processions were to meet at the basilica of Santa Maria Maggiore to chant a great litany. People were quite overcome and added their own prayers to the Kyrie eleisons. Then they thronged the streets on their way to St Peter's, and all went over the Pons Aelius where Gregory is said to have had a vision. He saw an angel sheathing his sword over the forbidding fortress – known ever after as the Castel Sant' Angelo – and the plague ceased.

Gregory was consecrated pope on 3 September AD590, being fifty years of age. By January 591 he could write: 'I have recovered a more cheerful frame of mind', and he set himself to the great tasks that came pouring in. There were letters concerning the war with the Lombards, whom he kept at bay with the aid of their devout Christian queen Theodelinda. The practical financial anxieties of the broken city became his responsibility more and more, pope though he was, and he found himself having to provide food, especially for the poor. The administration of both Church and Civil law fell to him, but his concern, above all, was with his endless letters as he established himself as the pastor and chief administrator of all priests, bishops and archbishops throughout Italy, Gaul and further afield. Finally he poured out so many moral, pastoral and scriptural treatises that he is called the fourth doctor of the Latin church. A new era was opening up. His beloved old imperial Rome was slowly changing under his rule into the majestic holy Roman Catholic and Apostolic Church of the middle ages; and it was to be a monkish world.

Britain under the old Roman Empire

The British Islands had once been a flourishing Christian country under the old Roman Empire. The Emperor Constantine had, in 311–2, been acclaimed as Augustus by his troops at York, and set off on his victorious march that was to lead to the battle of the Milvian Bridge near Rome in 312, to his conversion to Christianity and ultimately to his acceptance of the Nicene creed. Within a hundred years or so the Empire had become officially Christian. In 380 Constantine's ultimate successor, Emperor Theodosius the Great, had received baptism at the hands of bishop Ascholius and issued a decree in favour of St Peter and Pope Damasus of Rome. This was to be the true Christian Catholic faith, and the adherents of all other creeds were to be punished. By 390 all churches were to be surrendered to the Catholic bishops, and the Emperor overthrew the heathen temples 'throughout the whole world'. Christianity henceforth was to be established by force of arms with the aid of Roman generals and legionaries, and as far as Gaul and the British Islands were concerned, to be aided and abetted by the powerful spiritual or even physical violence of the almost legendary monk, Bishop Martin of Tours (316 – 397), often called the apostle of Gaul.

The policy had not really worked but it left deep roots, as the Goths, Huns, Franks, Vandals and Lombards had poured in. The Roman armies were defeated more and more often. Yet, even in Gregory's time, there were still pockets where the old Roman Empire held sway,

and he quickly used every possible opportunity by force of arms to put the heathen to flight and make the heretics feel the sting of the legionaries' whips. Gregory was an old fashioned Roman, dedicated to the ways of the Empire and ready to use force for the conversion of any laggardly pagans wherever the opportunity presented itself. He knew his gospel too well: 'Go to the open roads and hedgerows and *force* people to come in' (Luke 14, v. 23). Britain had once been a Roman Christian kingdom and he was ready to use every trick of diplomacy or subtle threats to win the Anglo–Saxon newcomers for Christ.

The visit of Agiulf from the city of Tours

It so happened that in those heady days in 590 when Gregory had been about to be consecrated as pope at the basilica of St Peter, there had arrived in Rome from Tours one called Agiulf, the personal deacon of the famous Bishop Gregory of Tours. If Rome and Constantinople had become the spiritual centres of the Empire, then the city of Tours with its basilica of St Martin had become the spiritual centre of Gaul under the encouragement of the whole Christian Frankish people. The deacon Agiulf had been sent for an audience with Pope Gregory to request some relics of the saints. This audience would provide for both of them an opportunity to discuss the state of the Frankish kingdom. Important clergymen like these, when they are full of their affairs of state and often in one another's studies or offices, love to have a heart to heart to share all that is going on in their own part of the world. The deacon had much to divulge to Pope Gregory about the Frankish people in a most vivid and readable way, for his Bishop, Gregory of Tours, was even at that moment working on what was later to become a real world best-seller called *The History of the Franks*, much of which was written in a day-to-day diary form.

If Pope Gregory had had time to read it through, or even to have listened to hear some of it read by the deacon Agiulf, it would immediately have made his famous papal hair curl more, for he could see now that the mission to Canterbury was at last definitely 'on'. He could visualise it all happening. The Frankish people, their senatorial bishops and their Merovingian royal family, muddle-headed and vicious as they could be, were all under the powerful spiritual influence of the long dead St Martin of Tours, a persona to be reckoned with throughout Gaul. He knew too that the tide of economic revival was in the air. He could see clearly how the missionaries could travel up the rivers Rhône, Saône and Loire to Tours, thence to Paris and the channel ports which were all wide open, and sail across the Channel to Canterbury. His personal secretary and spiritual brother with whom he had shared his visions, Augustine, might make an excellent leader. As soon as he had time, Pope Gregory started to send fulsome letters to the young king of the Franks, Childebert II, and even more importantly to the Queen Mother, Brunhilda, the real power in the land.

This meeting of Pope Gregory with the deacon Agiulf of Tours provides an excellent opportunity for Gregory of Tours (540–594) to make his entrance into our pilgrimage, for it is impossible to understand it without the use of his ten lively books *The History of the Franks*. Gregory (Bishop of Tours) gives an account in his history of the great litany over the Tiber which the deacon recorded on 5 April 590:

> At three o'clock all the choirs singing psalms came into the church, chanting the Kyrie eleison as they passed through the city streets. My deacon, who was present, said that while the people were making their supplication to the Lord, eighty individuals fell dead to the ground. The Pope never once stopped preaching to the people, nor did the people pause in their prayers. It was from [Pope] Gregory himself, while he was a deacon, that, as I have told you, my own deacon received the relics of the saints. Just as he was preparing to go into hiding, he was seized, carried along, brought to the basilica of St Peter, consecrated ready for his pontifical duties and then given to the City as Pope. My deacon could not resist turning back from Portus to witness the enthronement, for he wanted to see with his own eyes how the ceremony was carried out. (Gregory of Tours Book X.1)

At the beginning of our pilgrimage in Rome we will not be able to resist following that great rogation procession route which Pope Gregory had arranged so that all the faithful should travel from their chosen churches, walk over the Tiber and meet at the basilica of the Blessed Virgin Mary, Mother of our Lord Jesus Christ. In our minds we will join them as they thronged over the Tiber, and surely, when we see the dome of Hadrian's mausoleum, we shall remember the vision of the archangel Michael as he appeared sheathing his flaming sword to end the plague.

Saint Martin's tomb at Tours

CHAPTER TWO

More Characters to Meet

Bishop Gregory of Tours (AD 540–594)

GREGORY was born to the purple around AD 540 in Clermont-Ferrand in France. His great grandfather was from the old Gallo-Roman aristocracy and had been bishop of Langres. His ancestors included a number of saintly bishops. In the late fourth century the Gallo-Roman Christianity had been well established, largely through the dramatic missionary enterprise of the soldier-monk Bishop Martin of Tours (AD 316–397), but it had been thoroughly shaken as the Goths, Vandals, Visigoths and Franks had poured in, and all around was plunder, bloodshed, burning, looting and rape. Yet somehow the faithfulness of many bishops, priests, monks, nuns, hermits and laity had stood the test and had begun to attract many of their conquerors to Christianity.

At the age of eight Gregory was sent to school in the household of his uncle, Saint Gallus, Bishop of Clermont, and later to another uncle, an archdeacon Avitus. He seems to have been surrounded by his mother's churchy family of saintly uncles and aunts. He learnt his Latin well, read the first six books of the Aeneid, the Bible and especially Sulpitius Severus, the author who had known Bishop Martin personally. It was therefore no surprise when Gregory began to write fluently and even, from time to time, to burst into poesy. At the age of twenty-five Gregory was ordained deacon, but fell seriously ill. Like so many thousands from all over Gaul and even the British Isles, inspired by Sulpitius' life of St Martin, he made the pilgrimage to the saint's tomb at Tours for healing. To his joy he was miraculously healed. Inspired by the holiness of the place he stayed on there with Bishop Eufronius. The young man became so popular that when the bishop died in the year 573 the people of Tours, as a body, claimed him to be their new bishop at the age of thirty five.

Gregory was now a very important metropolitan bishop over the cathedral of Tours and eight other bishoprics. Above all he presided over St Martin's tomb at the basilica, now a great pilgrimage centre, where thousands from all over Gaul and Britain flocked for healing. It was a place on the high roads from North and South where people naturally exchanged news with one another about what was going on in the world. Apart from his highly disciplined liturgical life, he was now impossibly preoccupied with travelling, governing his beloved city of

Tours with great firmness, attending church synods (some of them contentious) and challenging the often wild Frankish royal families with their indisciplined and vicious habits. But when his day's work was over and his study door was shut, then he could take up his pen or quill or dictate by the hour to his shorthand writers on his real love, his books.

He started writing as a kind of journeyman theologian, learning his art as a hagiographer of the lives of the Fathers, with seven books of miracles to describe, then a commentary on the psalms and a book on the offices of the church; all solid pedestrian stuff. But then not long after his consecration he suddenly began to write from the heart. Old fashioned aristocratic Gallo-Roman though he was, he had come to love and admire the Franks, his conquerors, wild and crude as they were at times. He had come to look on them with an almost quizzical detachment, and was determined to write a full account of their history, from the beginning up to the present day.

The book began prosaically enough with Adam and Eve, then with résumés of the Old and New Testaments limping along piously, until he began to warm to Bishop Martin.

> At that period too our new luminary began to shine, and Gaul became bright with new rays coming from its lamps, for this is the moment when St Martin began to preach in this country. By his many miracles he overcame the disbelief of the gentiles and made it clear to the people that Christ, the Son of God, is himself the true God. He destroyed pagan temples, suppressed heresy, built churches and earned great renown for many miracles, crowning his claim to fame by restoring three dead men to life. (Gregory of Tours, Book I.39)

His narrative becomes more and more vivid and he hides nothing. By chapter six the narrative is so free and natural he is often dealing with day to day affairs in a diary form. Anyone setting out on this pilgrimage will have a rich experience as they read his *History of the Franks*, even if only by dipping into it. Ghastly murders, vicious tortures, plain lust, sexual wildness, rape, simple people left in cells to die without food, and all mixed up with heroic sanctity and kindness, and all the still sad music of humanity.

The Salian Franks were a Germanic people who originally lived in the region south of the Meuse, between that and the Scheldt. They were a people of great stature, with red or fair hair and they shaved themselves, leaving only 'soup cleaner' moustaches. Their kings and nobles let their hair grow long in a special way. They were ready, at the drop of the hatchet, to pick a quarrel and fight to the death with their sharp franciscas, or single edged axes or scramasaxes with short knives. Above all, after lust, they loved loot. The Romans had conquered them after many skirmishes and used their warriors as auxiliaries. After the great invasion in AD 406, when many tribes broke through the Rhine defences, it was the Franks who became the most powerful group in Gaul, led by the ruthless pagan King Clovis (466–511) who, as Gregory says, 'was a great man, and became a famous soldier' which was putting it mildly, as he was the founder of the Merovingian dynasty. One story in Gregory's book introduces us to King Clovis with his bloody axe. One day after a battle King Clovis had all the booty placed in a heap, and all were to take their agreed share. There was, however, a large ewer which Clovis felt was his by right, as king. All agreed, but one belligerent warrior, ready for a quarrel raised his battle axe, roared, and smashed the ewer. At the end of the year Clovis ordered the whole army to assemble on the parade ground and he inspected them. When he came to the man who had insulted him Clovis knocked down his axe as being filthy. The soldier knelt down to pick it up. Clovis raised his own battle axe in the air, brought it down and split his skull with it, and dismissed the rest of the parade. No wonder King Clovis waged many wars and won many victories.

King Clovis and Queen Clotild

Clovis, ruthless brigand though he was, was completely captivated and conquered by a gracious Christian woman, and their marriage was to have great consequences, not only for Frankish Gaul which was to be re-established as a Christian nation, but also for Augustine's mission, later, to the English people. Clovis the lusty conqueror had concubines, but at last decided that he needed to be properly wed, so he sent envoys to his neighbour, King Gundobad of Burgundy, as unscrupulous as himself, as Gregory's book continues:

> Clovis often sent envoys to Burgundy and they saw the girl Clotild. They observed that she was an elegant young woman and clever for her years, and they discovered that she was of the royal blood. They reported all this to Clovis and he immediately sent more messengers to Gundobad to ask for her hand in marriage. Gundobad was afraid to refuse and he handed Clotild over to them. They took her back with them, and presented her to their king. Clovis already had a son called Theuderic by one of his mistresses, but he was delighted when he saw Clotild and made her his wife.
>
> The first child which Clotild bore for Clovis was a son. She wanted to have her baby baptized, and she kept on urging her husband to agree to this. 'The gods whom you worship are no good,' she would say. 'They haven't even been able to help themselves, let alone others. They are carved out of stone or wood or some old piece of metal. The very names which you have given them were the names of men, not of gods. Take your Saturn, for example, who ran away from his own son to avoid being exiled from his kingdom, or so they say; and Jupiter, that obscene perpetrator of all sorts of mucky deeds, who couldn't keep his hands off other men, who had his fun with all his female relatives and couldn't even refrain from intercourse with his own sister (''*Jovisque et soror et coniunx*'' to quote her own words) What have Mars and Mercury ever done for anyone? They may have been edowed with magic arts, but they are certainly not worthy of being called divine. You ought instead to worship Him who created at a word and out of nothing heaven and earth, the sea and all that therein is, who made the sun to shine, who lit the sky with stars, who peopled the water with fish, the earth with beasts, the sky with flying creatures, at whose nod the fields became fair with fruits, the trees with apples, the vines with grapes, by whose hand the race of man was made, by whose gift all creation is constrained to serve in deference and devotion the man He made.' However often the Queen said this, the King came no nearer to belief. 'All these things have been created and produced at the command of our god,' he would answer. 'It is obvious that your God can do nothing and, what is more, there is no proof that he is a God at all.' (Gregory of Tours, Book II.28,29)

Queen Clotild gave birth to a son, but after its baptism it died, to Clovis' fury, for he felt that the God of Jesus Christ was really useless. Clotild then bore another son, Chlodomer, and she continued to pray that Clovis would be converted and be baptized one day. In the middle of a furious battle at a later date, when the troops of Clovis were being annihilated, Clovis suddenly looked up to heaven and cried out 'Jesus Christ, who Clotild maintains is the living God, give me your help, and if there is a miracle and we are saved I will be baptized'. Suddenly the enemy turned their backs on Clovis' army and ran away. Clovis, chastened, called for universal peace, and told Clotild what had happened.

This powerful, intelligent woman, full of simple grace and wit, with her well thought out Nicene or Catholic faith, persuaded her roughneck husband, like some obedient lap dog, to be baptized as a Christian:

> Like some new Constantine he stepped forward to the baptismal pool, ready to wash away the sores of his old leprosy and to be cleansed from the sordid stains, which he had borne so long. As he advanced for his baptism, the holy Man of God addressed him in these pregnant words: 'Bow your head in meekness, Sicamber' (viz. Merovingian). (Gregory of Tours, Book II.31)

Clearly Clovis really loved her, and she bore him five children.

As a result of new found Catholic beliefs, naive as they were, he became virtually king of most of Gaul. Gregory delights to show how Clovis and the Merovignian royal family were for ever to be devotees of St Martin, and his tomb at Tours was to be sacrosanct throughout Gaul to such an extent that it was as if St Martin's supernatural presence was there. Gregory's account gives an example of this:

> An army was assembled and Clovis marched on Poitiers. Some of his troops passed through land belonging to Tours. In respect for Saint Martin, Clovis ordered that they should requisition nothing in this neighbourhood except fodder and water. One of the soldiers found some hay belonging to a poor man. 'The King commanded that nothing should be requisitioned except fodder, didn't he?' said this man. 'Well, this is fodder. We shan't be disobeying his orders if we take it.' He laid hands on the poor man and took his hay by main force. This was reported to Clovis. He drew his sword and killed the soldier on the spot. 'It is no good expecting to win this fight if we offend Saint Martin,' he said. This was enough to ensure that the army took nothing else from this region. The King sent messengers to the church of Saint Martin. 'Off with you,' he said, 'and see if you can bring me some good tidings from God's House.' He loaded them with gifts which they were to offer to the church. 'Lord God,' said he, 'if You are on my side and if You have decreed that this people of unbelievers, who have always been hostile to You, are to be delivered into my hands, deign to show me a propitious sign as these men enter Saint Martin's church, so that I may know that You will support your servant Clovis.' The messengers set out on their journey and came to Tours as Clovis commanded. As they entered the church, it happened that the precentor was just beginning to intone this antiphon: 'For thou hast girded me with strength unto the battle: thou hast also given me the necks of mine enemies: that I might destroy them that hate me'. When the messengers heard this psalm, they gave thanks to God. They made their vows to the Saint and went happily back to report to the King. (Gregory of Tours, Book II.37)

The Roman Emperor Anastasius gave the newly Christian King Clovis the coveted Imperial Consulate, the receiving of which Clovis celebrated with great pomp.

In Saint Martin's church he stood clad in a purple tunic and the military mantle, and he crowned himself with a diadem. He then rode out on his horse and with his own hand showered gold and silver coins among the people present all the way from the doorway of Saint Martin's church to Tours cathedral. From that day on he was called Consul or Augustus. He left Tours and travelled to Paris, where he established the seat of his government. (Gregory of Tours, Book II.38)

Thus throughout Gaul, in spite of their wild and bloodthirsty family Merovingian ways to one another, and their careless cruelty to the peasantry, they always gave sanctuary in any building dedicated to St Martin, and gave protection to all bishops, priests, monks or hermits, except of course, to the most flagrantly crude or worldly. Gregory gives another example of how the Frankish people revered so completely St Martin of Tours. A hermit called Vulfolaic told Gregory of some miracles which St Martin had performed there:

A certain Frank, who came from a very noble family among his own people, had a son who was deaf and dumb. The boy was brought by his parents to this church, and I ordered him to sleep on a bed in the building itself, at the side of my deacon and another of my priests. All day long he busied himself with prayer, and at night time, as I have told you, he slept in the church. God took pity on him and Saint Martin appeared to me in a vision. 'You can now move your protegé out of the building,' he said, 'for he is cured.' The next morning, as I was thinking about the vision which I had seen, the boy came up to me and spoke. His first words were to give thanks to God for what had happened. Then he turned to me and said, 'I am thanking Almighty God for having given me my speech and my hearing'. He

then went back home for he was completely cured. (Gregory of Tours, Book VIII.16)

It is strange indeed how many Christians nowadays are finding miraculous healing coming to them from the charismatic speaking in tongues, in much the same way as in Gregory's descriptions; the dead were raised, the deaf could hear, the blind see, etc, only not from the Spirit, but from St Martin himself, bringing the crowds from near and far to touch the Saint's tomb at Tours for miracles, and not being disappointed.

Saint Martin of Tours

It is not necessary here to describe fully the strange life of St Martin of Tours, who made such a profound impression on the Frankish people, for I have written of him fully in my book *Martin of Tours, Parish Priest, Mystic and Exorcist*. The bare bones of the story are that Martin was born in AD 316, the son of a high ranking officer in the Roman army. At the age of fifteen he was, by force, conscripted as a young officer. One winters day at Amiens he met a beggar and gave him half of his cloak. In a dream Martin saw himself giving the cloak to Jesus and this led to his baptism and to his taking up, eventually, non-combatant duties. When his military service was over he became a hermit in a ruined villa near Poitiers. After ten years of godly silence, a group of young hermits joined him, and miracles began to happen around him. Moved by his sanctity, the people of Tours grabbed him by trickery and made him their bishop. He retired to a shack near the flat plain of the Loire, below the caves at Marmoutier, where a

Martin when he left
the army / from a mural
by Simone Memmi 1284-1344
in the lower church of Assisi

whole crowd of young ardent hermits, both male and female, gathered so that the first monastery of the west was founded. Out of his long silences, Martin was eventually driven with his young men to go on missions in the neighbourhood to convert the heathen. He knocked down sacred temples, fought with the devil, healed the sick, and regardless of fear, confronted the secular authorities demanding social justice for the poor and the oppressed. In 397 in the church at Candes as he lay quietly on a straw mattress dying he suddenly cried to the devil 'Why do you stand there you bloody monster . . . Abraham's bosom is about to receive me . . .' and so died.

There still remains something very profound about his life, for the books by the young advocate Sulpitius Severus, who knew him well, slightly garrulous though he may have been at times, are not the work of a hagiographer. Rather, he writes like a perceptive novelist. Be that as it may, it was Martin who fired the spiritual imagination of Benedict himself, and left a trail, not only in Gaul, but even more powerfully in Ireland and Britain. Wherever we travel in our pilgrimage we shall find churches dedicated to Martin and it is strange how deeply he worked into the very bones of western Europe. In the old Book of Common Prayer, Martin is the only saint to have two festivals all to himself (apart from the Blessed Virgin Mary and John the Baptist), one on the 4th July and the other on 11th November. My magnificent embossed volume *Saint Martin*, by A. Lecoy de la Marche, lists in France 3,674 churches, many bridges, monasteries, schools and commercial undertakings bearing the name of St Martin. There are also many other churches and establishments in Germany, the Netherlands and Britain bearing the same dedication and it is of little surprise to find hidden under them the remains of old Roman shrines and villas.

When King Clovis and Queen Clotild died their booty was divided among their four sons, and for the next hundred years Gregory describes how life was extremely difficult for ordinary people. One petty kingdom battled with another, there were the cruel garrotings, the rack, vicious torture, the burning of homes, prisoners left in dungeons to die without food or water, others buried alive, and above all the cruelty of deliberately watching innocent people die in agony. There it all is in Gregory's ten volumes, and it is against this backdrop that St Augustine and his companions were to travel. It is possible to leave out much of the misery, though Gregory makes a splendid story of it all, and there are some people who come out clearly into the pilgrimage, as the following explains.

Of Clovis' and Clotild's four sons, Lothar I won the day after internecine warfare. Then, apart from the concubines he kept, he took to himself a wife called Queen Radigund, but she quickly became disgusted with him, became a nun and eventually a well known abbess near Poitiers. He married Queen Ingund, who bore him five sons. He then turned his attentions on Ingund's sister, Aregund. He took her off to the villa where she lived, slept with her, and married her as well! From this incontinent behaviour, by Lothar's progeny came much desperate misery for many millions in the following generations. Gregory neatly describes him: 'he was too much given to woman chasing'. Lothar was, in the end, however, ashamed of himself and made the pilgrimage to St Martin's tomb. There he confessed all his dirty deeds, and prayed for Martin to help him. He went off hunting, fell ill of a fever and died, complaining to St Martin: 'Would you believe it? What sort of God of heaven is this, to finish off a great monarch like me in this way?' On Lothar's death, four of his sons, Charibert, Guntram, Chilperic and Sigibert then divided the estate between themselves.

King Charibert, Queen Ingoberg and their daughter the Princess Bertha of Canterbury

Charibert, King of Paris, was the most dissolute and savage of them all. He pillaged far and wide with his troops and, like his father's 'woman chasing' habits, had at least three concubines. He decided at last that he should take to himself a real wife, and chose as his royal bride one Ingoberg, a most refined and pious woman. She bore him a daughter who was to be none other than our own Queen Bertha of Canterbury. Queen Ingoberg found that playing second, third and fourth fiddle to Charibert's insulting concubines was too much, so she aggravated him and in the end he sent her packing. She retired to a house in the Tours area and lived in a religious way and brought up her daughter Bertha as befitted the saintly granddaughter of the famous Clotild, who had converted the Frankish people to Christianity. Bertha was nurtured in an atmosphere of calmness and quiet gentility. There were, it seems, many large houses and mansions around Tours where wealthy women like Ingoberg, 'grass' or real widows, lived in semi-religious seclusion, more than happy to be far away from their drunk and lascivious Merovingian erstwhile husbands. They often had a chapel with priests to take the services each day if they wished to attend. They had a host of indoor and outdoor servants which enabled them to live an undisturbed life of ease. They had their lap dogs and their tapestry frames, the entertainment of sometimes watching the hunt, and the care of the poor and sick by visiting them. Of course everything was under the guardianship of St Martin. Gregory of Tours describes how he was visited by Queen Ingoberg, then aged seventy. He greatly admired her and helped her to make her will, leaving legacies to Tours and Le Mans cathedrals and to St Martin's church. She died suddenly, and freed many of her serfs. I often wonder whether she had, from time to time taken ship over the Channel to see her daughter. In the end King Charibert's matrimonial affairs brought on himself much anger, ending in his excommunication. He died in 567.

Queen Brunhilda and Queen Fredegund

If the Merovingian kings on the whole were a scurrilous group with little political skill or diplomacy, and when arguing with an opponent could use a direct hit on the head with one of their scramasaxes or daggers, or use the rack or some other shameful cruelty, towards their women they could behave quite differently. People like Queen Clotild or Ingoberg or the Princess Bertha were very very good. But now two powerful irascible women were about to appear on the stage of the whole of Gaul, Queen Brunhilda and Queen Fredegund, who was not only nasty but could behave intolerably. Soon, with their wild kings and families they had the place in an uproar. From the period of Pope Gregory's enthronement in 590 to the setting out of Augustine's mission from St Andrews monastery on the Caelian Hill for Canterbury in 596 these two women virtually ruled Frankish Gaul, living at daggers drawn to one another and each determined to oust the other and become regent of the whole kingdom.

Sigibert, King of Austrasia, one of Lothar's sons, settled at Rheims and married Queen Brunhilda, daughter of King Athanagild. She was a charming character, lovely and chaste and she spoke well. She was converted from Arianism to become a devout Catholic, became a great admirer of St Martin of Tours, and she bore a child called Childebert I. King Chilperic, whose capital was at Soissons, was a despicable person, a very Nero or Herod. He had his concubines and he married Queen Andovera, but then fell in love with Queen Brunhilda's sister Galswinth as well. She displeased him so he had her garotted by one of his servants! His favours then fell on Fredegund, a serving woman, an incredibly unpleasant character who was arrogantly determined to win the whole kingdom for herself and her husband. Without compunction she, in cold blood, paid two young warriors to kill King Sigibert with poisoned scramasaxes, and they were successful. She then sent off a cleric to assassinate Queen Brunhilda which, fortunately for Brunhilda, failed.

In 584 King Chilperic was mysteriously assassinated, so these two powerful women were at one another's throats, literally, at any rate as far as Queen Fredegund was concerned. She was determined to rule over Frankish Gaul and become Queen regent for her infant son, Lothar II. Gaul was in uproar; Fredegund was callous and devilish to all who crossed her. She stopped at nothing; garotting and murder was child's play. Sexual licence, poisoning and even apparently conniving at the murder, on Easter Day, of Bishop Praetextatus and watching him as he bled to death. Several times, it seems, she attempted to assassinate Queen Brunhilda and her son Childebert II. When to her consternation her own young son Lothar II was ill, even to the point of death and her whole grand design was about to collapse around her, it was she who in desperation sent a large donation to St Martin's tomb at Tours, and when the child recovered Gregory näively commented: 'That is why he recovered'.

Fredegund had a perpetual grudge

against her rather repulsive daughter, Rigunth. One day she invited Rigunth to open her father's chest of jewels, and said 'do what you like with them, they're all yours'. The girl gloated over them and while stretching over it all, her mother suddenly slammed the chest lid over the girl's throat, until her eyes stood out of her head. In the end the servants separated the two women. In this way much ill feeling spread throughout the land and existed between the two women. Fredegund was a real Jezebel, but in the end she died peacefully in bed with her vision of the united kingdom of the Franks unfulfilled. This was in 597, the very year when Augustine and his party were travelling through her area. She had to leave her child-king Lothar II to the tender mercies of her hated enemy Queen Brunhilda, her sister-in-law.

In the meantime Queen Brunhilda had managed to live a charmed life, being chased from pillar to post to avoid the machinations of Queen Fredegund, and even at one time seeking sanctuary in the basilica by St Martin's tomb where she stayed. But she was of a different calibre. She had the most statesmanlike approach to her kingdoms of Austrasia and Burgundy, as can be seen from the Treaty of Andelot. She was helped by Bishop Gregory himself. She had the same sort of vision of uniting the whole Frankish nation as Fredegund, only with much more likelihood of achieving it, especially when she was left, in 597, virtually as regent of the whole kingdom with three young adolescent boys – Lothar II and her own two grandsons Theudebert and Theuderic, to exert her influence. She could see, like the Emperor Constantine before her, that the Catholic Church was a most powerful influence for the unity

of a nation; and chose with skill suitable candidates for bishoprics. She used, too, all her statecraft to establish castles and roads to provide a network for the army and for travellers, for her embassies and for missionaries on their way, busy to keep the Christian vision alive far and wide. Even to this day her enduring work is remembered as her roads are called 'Les chaussées de Brunhild'.

At this point, with her rival out of the way, Brunhilda realised that, with Pope Gregory, a new era was emerging, and to her delight she started to receive flattering letters from him. She could see now that it was a moment of great mutual advantage, for at last there seemed a real possibility for the grand vision of a united Frankish Gaul to take place, underpinned by the Catholic Church and strengthened by the fresh vitality of Pope Gregory. On the other hand Gregory could see that now was his chance to start taking the Frankish bishops to task about the lax and sometimes sordid ways that he had heard of from Bishop Gregory of Tours, from the talk with the deacon Agiulf, and the ten books on the *History of the Franks*, and many other reports. Pope Gregory could see too, that with Fredegund out of the way, there was a real breathing space for Frankish Gaul. The relationship between them ripened through correspondence. Pope Gregory was not merely being the polite diplomat, for he had a visible affection for the game widow Brunhilda. He could write letters like this to her about her son Childebert II:

> Gregory to Brunhilda, Queen of the Franks, [and every sentence must have sounded music to her ears] 'The laudable and God-blessing goodness of your excellence is manifested both by your

government of your kingdom and by your education of your son.

The Presbyter Candidus

Pope Gregory in the meantime had been sending out personal apostolic vicars to various parts of the world with power to negotiate on his behalf, to keep him informed of what was going on, and generally to encourage his enterprises. One of these was a Roman presbyter, a man of some importance called Candidus. It was his pleasant task to give the pallium personally to Syagrius, Brunhilda's favourite bishop. The coveted pallium was a stole, in the shape of a yoke, given by the pope himself as a sign of gratitude for good work done, and Brunhilda and her bishop were no doubt delighted. The arrival of Candidus in Marseilles certainly signified the wind of change in Gaul, for Gregory went on to sack the Bishop of Arles' agent who had been, it seems, lazily squandering a piece of land that rightly belonged to the papacy, and demanded that Candidus should take over the estate and hand over the revenues owing. Brunhilda was thoroughly primed and ready to help Gregory, with the matter of the revenues settled, and he sent this letter to the presbyter Candidus on his way to the estates in Gaul. He wrote in a rather stilted and involved style compared to Gregory of Tours' racy narrative.

> be so good as to buy as soon as possible garments that are worn by the poor, and also English boys, of the age of seventeen or eighteen years, that they may be given to God in the monasteries, to their profit ... and, as we said before, boys who may profit in the service of almighty God. But as those who are to be had in that country are heathens, I desire that a presbyter should be sent over with them, for fear of sickness occurring on the journey, in order that if he sees any likely to die, he may duly baptize them. (Mason. p. 17)

These boys were the mythical 'angels' appearing at last in the flesh for Gregory. How strange it also is that Gregory writes: 'that a presbyter should *be sent over* with them' using the strange word 'transmittatur'. Cannot one see these seventeen and eighteen year olds, bought up as slaves in the market at Rome, being carefully weeded out and vetted and 'transmittatur', sent over, to the great monastic island of Lérins, and then set free from their slavery to finish their training there, ready to join Augustine and the forty companions when they arrived from Rome.

The enthusiasm for the preparations was mounting at St Andrews on the Caelian Hill and in the curia, and in the midsummer of 596 Pope Gregory was busy writing the famous 'letters commendatory' to Brunhilda, to her two grandsons King Theudebert and King Theuderic, to the Emperor's patrician of Gaul, to the Frankish bishops and the monks at the famous monastery at Lérins. He asked them all to give the travellers a good welcome in every ecclesiastical diocese, to 'help them with prayer and other aids', which meant give them lodging and food, a posse of legionaries to protect them, and the boats or wagons needed for all the baggage required. In our pilgrimage we too shall follow the way indicated by Gregory's 'letters commendatory' as they take us from Lérins up the Rhône, the Saône, and down the Loire to Tours. They need not detain us now, but the *coup de grace* that Gregory had been so carefully preparing for Brunhilda certainly deserves to be reported in preparation for our visit to Chalon, her capital. Pope Gregory in his letter greeted Brunhilda fulsomely with a father's love. He told her how the English nation longed to be Christian, but that the priests in the neighbourhood had no pastoral care for the people. Therefore he was sending Augustine, whose zeal and earnestness he knew well, with some companions, to effect their conversion. He was to bring with him presbyters for he knew how the Queen longed to see the English nation converted, and he was sure that she would help in every way with her patronage to the fullest extent. This group of letters finally completed in July 596 went, it seems, personally with the 'presbyter sent over with them' from Rome. These letters ensured that 'Augustine, bearer of these presents' did not arrive anywhere unannounced, for if such a large group with its posse of soldiers and all its baggage were to go from one bishop or royal palace to the next without the proper previous diplomatic overtures, they would be most unwelcome. When, therefore, these letters arrived in Gaul, the energetic Candidus had before him a time of feverish activity as he delivered them to their destinations in advance of the group's arrival. He also needed to make all the preparations for the party when it eventually arrived.

St Augustine of Canterbury

All that needed to be done now was to choose the monks who were to go on the expedition, and their leader. Monks do not like moving from one place to another and there was much apprehension as to who should go. In theory the common vote of the community under the abbot had to make such a choice. Although Gregory was no longer abbot it was very clear that it was he who was behind the choosing of the men from his own beloved community at St Andrew's on the Caelian Hill. He chose Augustine, his own syncellus or cell mate, to be their leader and prior. Augustine had originally trained as a student under the rather cunning Bishop Felix of Messina before becoming a monk of St Andrew's. Gregory had been attracted by Augustine's helpful and pliant obedience and had successfully trained him to become prior of his large monastery. After his elevation to the papacy Gregory had then accepted Augustine as his personal friend and confidant, so his choice as mission leader was a foregone conclusion. Augustine was no dynamic character, unlike his master. He was more of a civil servant kind of person, shrewd and cautious, very tall, haughty and pompous but at times timid, afraid of giving offence to his master and above all subservient. However, he was a good team maker as it eventually transpired, and after a while the group was assembled – Laurence, Honorius the precentor, Jacob the deacon, Paulinus and John, some forty in all.

The arrangements for the journey had now to be made, and it was no small project. This was not a group of wandering friars as in a later age, begging their way from place to place, and ready to sleep under hedges. These civilised monks were more like a large group of well-to-do refugees who were planning to settle, bag and baggage, in Canterbury. Wagons and ships were necessary. There were piles of daily clothing, all the vestments for the liturgy, the many

Sketch of
Gregory the Great with St Augustine from a
12th century mosaic in Cefalu cathedral

manuscripts needed for the chanting of the liturgy each day, the great silver cross which was to be unveiled at Thanet, and a great ikon of Jesus in glory which was to lead them through Gaul. There were gifts and relics from the saints at Rome as tokens for these who welcomed them at each stage. All these and other odds and ends were eventually gathered, and the departure was set for some time in July or August 596.

Pope Gregory then gave a missionary benediction to the group as they stood in St Andrew's on the Caelian Hill. This spot is today marked with a plaque to commemorate this important occasion all those years ago.

We shall never know what route they took as they set off. All we know is that they went to work in obedience to the Pope's command. They had but accomplished a small portion of the journey when meeting a wild and fierce tribe, they thought of going home. However they decided to send Augustine back to Pope Gregory personally, telling him the mission was impossible. In his own words, Gregory gave Augustine and the group one of those great blistering tickings off that change the world:

GREGORY, SERVANT OF THE SERVANTS OF GOD, TO THE SERVANTS OF OUR LORD
It would have been better not to begin good things, than, when they are begun, to turn back from them again in thought; and therefore, dearest sons, you should earnestly endeavour to accomplish the good work which with the Lord's help you have begun. Do not allow yourselves to be deterred by the toilsomeness of the journey, nor by the tongues of evil-speaking men; but with all determination and enthusiasm finish under the blessing of God, what you you have taken up, knowing that great toil is followed by greater glory of the eternal recompense. (Bede, Book I.23)

After delivering this rebuke Pope Gregory merely appointed Augustine as abbot to strengthen his authority, and told him not to be so chicken hearted. This first failure of the mission demands some understanding, for my guess is that the *small* portion of the journey and the 'uncivilised, a fierce and an unbelieving nation' were not the Britons at all, but the hated Lombards who were, despite Pope Gregory's best endeavours, still following their old lifestyle of ravaging, looting, raping and general mayhem.

The Lombards were a Germanic tribe in origin, whom Pope Gregory called the 'unspeakable, abominable heretics'; some of them were Arians who denied that Jesus was divine, and many were plain pagans. In 568 they had swept through northern Italy, Milan and the Po Valley,' Umbria and Tuscany, and under their King Authari (531–591) they were gradually approaching Rome, bent on sacking the city where Pope Gregory had been

made pope in 590. In 591, as he walked round the city, he had had the horror of seeing the spirals of smoke rising from the plundered villages outside the walls, and the Italian prisoners of war tethered to the walls, waiting to be sold in the markets. He had wept when his own captured soldiers were sent into the city with their hands cut off, in humiliation. However, once again Pope Gregory had been able to change the whole course of history with the aid of one of his charming and dynamic lady friends. The story of Theodelinda, Queen of the Lombards is full of romance. King Authari is reputed to have sought his bride, the daughter of Garibaldi, Duke of the Bavarians, by first going in disguise to her father's court to see her, and then being quite captivated by her beauty. She was an extremely devout, fully Nicene Christian, though a member of the mildly non-conformist (three chapter) group, of which Gregory did not at all approve, but was prepared to suffer in silence. Shortly after their marriage Authari died, in 591, at the gates of the city of Rome. The Lombard nobles, a most argumentative group, asked in council if their charming young queen would choose one of their number to be their king. She chose Agilulf, the Duke of Turin, an Arian who seemed more compliant and not quite such a 'loathe-some and filthy man' as the others.

In 591 Agilulf moved in on to the city of Rome itself demanding admission, and a large sum of money to be paid as ransom. Pope Gregory admitted him. The two men came face to face on the steps of St Peter's, one the stern monk who spent hours in contemplation, keeping under control his iron will, and the other, the wild 'nefandissimus', the execrable Lombard with his motley crew. Pope Gregory outcountenanced them all with disdain, gave the five hundred pounds of gold they demanded, and they sheepishly slunk back to Milan, their headquarters.

At Monza, near Milan, Theodelinda worshipped with her devout Catholic court circle at their basilica of St John the Baptist. Her pliable husband King Agilulf encouraged this devotion and won many Arians and pagans to Catholic ways though he himself was never converted. Gregory realised that it had been the timely death of Theodelinda's first husband that made Agilulf, her new husband and King, lift the the siege of Rome and usher in a new climate where the pope 'the servant of the servants of God', was seen to be becoming the most powerful pontiff. Gregory started to send her charming gifts which won the hearts of the court admirers; a copy of his own dialogues, a jewelled gospel book and what is believed to be a most exquisite hen and seven chicks wrought in silver gilt.

It is possible that Augustine's group set off first along the coastal Via Aurelia to Genoa, Nice and Lérins, where they would have been under the protection of the Exarchate at Ravenna. The next part of the journey would be through Lombard territory where, although Agilulf and Theodelinda were now in control, there was not entire freedom from the possibility of marauding Lombard warlords with their raiding bands. Augustine halted at, let us say, Piombino on the edge of Lombard territory, where he heard gruesome tales of looting and ravaging by these warlords. He was sent back to Rome saying that the road was impassable and that the whole project could not go ahead. Pope Gregory was thoroughly annoyed in spite of his usual encouraging

attitude, and sent Augustine, now their abbot and under servile obedience, to charter a ship and make direct for the island of Lérins, a few miles from Nice. It certainly seems to have been a sound solution, and will be for the modern pilgrim. There is a ferry from Piombino to Bastia, then on to Nice where one can travel by the local boats to Lérins.

King Ethelbert Queen Bertha and Bishop Liudhard

When King Charibert of Paris, sometime between the years 550–558 had deeply insulted his Queen Ingoberg and in fury sent her packing, virtually divorced, she had made for the area between Tours and le Mans, where she had a special devotion for St Martin of Tours and the saint's tomb. With her daughter the Princess Bertha, she lived a quiet and religious life there. The Princess Bertha was brought up in the tradition of her great-grandmother Queen Clotild (died 544) and was groomed for the day when she would be ready to marry a king as tough as old King Clovis had been, and bring him to heel as a Christian. As Gregory of Tours in his books makes it clear the times for the Catholic Church were changing fast, for out of the old Roman Christian culture a quite new style of life was emerging. The Merovingian kings, lusty and often bestial though they were, were beginning to see the great benefits that would come to them from the growing numbers of a literate clergy and the religious orders. Marriage to a civilised and cultured spouse often brought with it not only wealth in the shape of a handsome dowry, but also new and advantageous political affiliations with powerful neighbours.

Some time in 558 there came an embassy from the young Prince Ethelbert of

Kent, then some thirty years old, seeking the Princess Bertha in marriage. Ethelbert was originally of the Saxon royal family, descended from the almost mythical Hengist. There had been much intermarriage between the Saxons and the Jutes, who had especially close connections with the Franks. Their style of land management was similar and there have been unearthed a whole range of Frankish weapons and brooches in Kent. Queen Ingoberg immediately insisted, with her husband Charibert of Paris, that if their daughter was to be wed in such an apparently god-forsaken country, the Princess Bertha should be allowed to carry on her worship as a Christian, to have a small church or chapel to worship in with her family; and to have a presbyter to conduct the Eucharist there regularly. The permission was gladly given, for Ethelbert and many of his father's nobles certainly wanted the benefit of a Christian culture and to have the establishment of the rule of statutory law, even if they did not wish to give up their old religious practices. As a result the young princess was given a large chapel, built upon the ruins of a Roman church, house or oratory, as a present for her marriage. In addition the child bride princess had the delight, besides the company of her presbyter, of her own bishop, Liudhard, a Frank. She was able to begin her quiet mission to convert the people, while he could baptize, anoint, give the sacrament and ordain clergy when the time was ripe.

In 560; Ethelbert was appointed as King of Kent, and after a number of vicious wars, gradually, on account of his skill in warfare and statesmanship, became accepted as Bretwalda, or pre-eminent king of the chiefs from Kent to Humber. In 596 the news began to percolate through Gaul that Augustine and his companions were on their way. Bede's account now becomes lyrical. It is not that the picture becomes merely a figment of his imagination, as if the Merovingian kings and queens were all set out as dark and evil, while the English scene, by contrast, was all bright and easy. There are certain epochs to which people look back on as if life for the generality of people had been reasonably good, and where the King was known as the kindest of men and his wife a worthy consort.

On our pilgrimage when we land at Thanet and stand by St Augustine's cross at Ebbsfleet we can savour that famous moment which Bede describes so vividly (Book I.25). In the meantime we will read a shortened version of the letter that Pope Gregory, that arch convincer of lively and intelligent women, wrote to our godly Queen Bertha which must have brought to her, her husband and the English people, much joy. 'To Bertha, Queen of the English', Gregory writes. He then relates how the presbyter Lawrence and the monk Peter, on their return to Rome, had told him of the great encouragement shown by Bertha towards Augustine and his mission in Canterbury. He often refers to her as 'illustrious lady' and likens her to the mother of Constantine 'the ever memorable Helen' in her enthusiasm in causing many to accept baptism and for having 'predisposed the mind' of her husband Ethelbert to follow the Gospel teaching. He exhorts her to keep up her powerful influence, through prayer, over the English people so that they may go on from strength to strength. He closes expressing the hope that her reward and that of her husband will be 'that you may reign here happily' and 'after many years may receive also the joys of the life to come, which know no end.' (Mason. p. 57)

Church of Reconciliation
Taizé

CHAPTER THREE

The Unexpected Saint

HAVING read Bede's account of the mission from Rome to Canterbury, and also enjoyed St Gregory of Tours' often quite scurrilous account with its racy tabloid narrative, and armed with Pope Gregory's obsequious diplomatic effusions to the bishops, kings and queens of Gaul, I was all ready in my mind to start my pilgrimage. At St Andrew's on the Caelian Hill I would ask for a missionary benediction and then set off for the journey to Canterbury. Suddenly there appeared out of the blue what I can only call a joker in the pack. Here was this extraordinary Irish monk, Columban (the dove), with twelve disciples, walking straight across the course of Augustine's path.

How they never met seems most odd. Our local library was quick to help me with the *Dictionary of National Biography* and even more excitingly, to send me the small modern, scholarly paperback called *Columbanus in his own words* by Tomas O Fiaich, Cardinal Archbishop of Armagh, who wrote to me full of appreciation for my book on St Martin.

Now if Augustine and his monks seemed rather a businesslike yet colourless team, Columban and his companions were exactly the opposite, for they all had charisma with a capital 'C'. As Tomas O Fiaich writes:

> Columban was Ireland's first European, poet, scholar, abbot, preacher, saint, co-founder (with St Martin) of western monasticism, associate of kings, correspondent of popes, he was the centre of controversy in his own day, and has gone on generating argument ever since.

Columban was born in 543 at Leinster and in his youth had an outstandingly beautiful face and his character was so full of charm that women loved him. He gave himself unquestioningly to Christ, hook, line and sinker and determined to live as a monk after the example of St Martin, needing no money and very basic clothing only. Like all the Irish, Welsh and Scots monks he adopted the style of a partly shaved head. The sight of fair women trying to catch him caused in Columban a wild battle to control his personal sexual desire, almost to madness. He spent hours in solitude and by the time he was forty two he had won a kind of victory over his desires. Now, instead of attracting women by his beauty, he began to attract men by his sanctity and he taught them the passionate love of Jesus Christ and the power of chastity. He formed a small community of twelve disciples determined, like Jesus, to convert the world. At first they landed in Cornwall, but their hearts were set on converting the Frankish people to a more godly and spiritual frame of mind. They took ship and landed in Gaul, sometime between 590–593. King Guntram, captivated by the holiness of Columban and his group, offered them the ruins of a Roman fort in the Haute-Saône area, called Angrates, and there they settled, living sometimes only on herbs and the bark of trees. They found a ruined temple dedicated to the goddess Diana which they rebuilt with their own hands and consecrated to St Martin of Tours.

The sanctity of Columban and his twelve monks became so famous that great crowds of young men flocked to him and his brothers, captivated by their chanting. It must have been rather like the young and old who today are enraptured by the great gatherings for chanting at Taizé, near Cluny, and the deep silences. In 593 King Guntram died and handed over his kingdom to the young Childebert II, whose bossy queen Mother Brunhilda, Pope Gregory's special lady wire puller, was already the power behind the throne. Attracted by the news, Childebert gave permission to Columban to open a larger monastery at Luxeuil, eight miles away, and then to build yet another at Fontaine, three miles north of it. Queen Mother Brunhilda gave them a great welcome because she could see the economic advantages to be gained from using the virtually voluntary slavery of the monks, working for no pecuniary gain, to clear the wild forest and make it into a place of delight and future profit. She had a religious infatuation with clergymen, monks and nuns, especially those of a subservient nature, but now, in Columban she had more than met her match and would soon rue the day of their meeting.

Columban remained, like St Martin, an attractive and completely unusual person. Often he would go off with only one follower to spend 'listening' days in solitude among the trees. Birds would alight on his shoulder and he might caress them, and squirrels would run down and nestle in his cowl. On the other hand he was wildly headstrong and when the 'prophesying' was on him, nothing would halt him. Like St Martin he would tear down pagan temples with his own bare hands, and set them on fire. His fellow monks often had on these occasions to usher him off somewhere else for his own safety. To him prophecy, visions, poesy and the recitation of the psalms were all so akin that he would sometimes spontaneously burst into lyrical song, such as the time when he and the brothers were rowing up the Rhine against the swift stream:

> 'Heia viri! nostrum reboans
>   echo sonet, heia!
> Heave ho, my lads! Heave ho! Our echoes
>   rebound around. Heave ho!'

He had his own quaint rule and sometimes treated his brothers as if they were naughty children. His punishment of them took the form of slapping which quickly became slapstick at times. 'The one who shall forget the prayer before work or after work – with twelve blows', 'for anyone who through coughing goes wrong in the chant at the beginning of a psalm . . . six blows' or 'the one who smiles at the office of prayers – with six blows: if he bursts out laughing aloud – with a grave penance unless *it happens excusably*!' He preached quaint sermons in pedantic Latin and his letters to novices, bishops or popes make curious reading, especially when he wrote at length and frequently about the date of Easter, a matter which seemed to be so vital to the Celtic saints. But when he was 'in prophecy' he must have been quite devastating.

The regent queen Mother Brunhilda, at the height of her power, was staying with her two adolescent sons Theudebert and Theuderic at Bourcheresse. It happened that Columban, who was on his travels, was near, so she asked him to visit her. He entered the hall in one of his most devastatingly prophetic moods, as if Elijah were confronting Jezebel, and asked what she wanted of him. Queen Brunhilda held out the two boy kings to him, both of whom were born out of wedlock to concubines, and with regal arrogance said: 'These are the king's sons. Strengthen them with your blessing'. Thoroughly roused by the spirit of prophecy in him Columban cried: 'Know this, these two boys shall never hold the kingly sceptre, for they are the offspring of the stews'.

Columban led to Tours

The queen never forgave him and hounded him from one end of her kingdom to the other, especially as he repeatedly declared that the two young kings would soon both be dead. Hated by the royal families he and his group wandered all over Europe, never able to settle until, eventually in despair he was led, like a homing pigeon, to Tours. There in the basilica by St Martin's tomb he spent a whole night in desperate prayer to the saint. The next day he came out of the experience filled with a blind fury, like St Martin himself who used to rage at all those who were maltreating the downtrodden and desperate. The local bishop invited him to dinner, and at the meal Columban cried out insolently: 'It is that dog Theuderic who has torn me from my brethren'. When one of King Theuderic's

aunts remonstrated, Columban said: 'Go, tell him that within three years he and his sons will perish'. One of the courtiers said: 'Is this the speech of a man of God? Why do you use such words?' Columban tersely answered: 'Because I cannot keep silent of the words that the Lord has given me to speak'.

He and his companions were eventually told to pack their bags and go back home to Ireland as they had become such a nuisance. They sailed off down the Loire towards Saint Nazaire, but a storm carried the ship back ashore. Eventually the ship's captain re-floated the vessel and deposited them again on the shore of Gaul. After many adventures it seemed as if Divine Providence was beckoning him to Italy, so Columban, now aged seventy, took his beloved pilgrim's staff and with his companions climbed over the Alps and down into Italy, to Milan, where a rapturous welcome awaited them from queen Theodelinda, her husband Agilulf and their court. Here at last, with them, Columban and his group found refuge and peace. King Agilulf gave him a piece of land high up in the valley of the Trebbia where there was a ruined church in the village of Bobbio dedicated to St Peter. There were two caves in the hills above the village where they could retire in retreat. There was a great deal of manual work of reconstruction to do and the whole community, including Columban, set to work vigorously. The community flourished and did much to help Theodelinda's work to win the Arian Lombards to Nicene Catholic Christianity. Many monasteries sprang up throughout Europe, founded by Columban's disciples, all with their own quaint rule and their particular Irish style of Celtic piety. Eventually, over the years, most were merged into those of the Benedictine or Cistercian orders. To this day the effect of his work has been immeasurable throughout the world, and there are still many Irish convents or communities who look to his rule for their guidance.

There is a most unsavoury postcript to Columban's prophecy to Queen Brunhilda about her young charges, the same Brunhilda who had done so much to encourage Augustine and his companions on their mission to Canterbury; for by the year 612–3 both kings Theudebert and Theuderic were dead, as Columban had prophesied. King Lothar II, their cousin, was in charge of the whole of Frankish Gaul, and his aunt Brunhilda had become increasingly authoritarian over the years. Now she was completely at his mercy. She was arrested and flogged before King Lothar's troops, stripped naked and exhibited on a camel's back for three days, after which she was tied by her hair to the tail of a wild stallion. As some sort of belated compensation her ashes are now preserved in the abbey at Autun, which is dedicated to St Martin who had done so much to influence her eventful life. Columban died in the early hours of Sunday 23 November 615 at the age of seventy two in one of his caves above Bobbio. His body rests under the basilica there.

Of all this list of *dramatis personae* alive and influential at the eventful time around 596 when the great English pilgrimage from Rome to Canterbury was being planned and executed, the one who seems unexpectedly to have taken centre stage is the joker of the pack, the captivating Columban. He is hardly mentioned in the English story, yet here he was with his own freelance pilgrimage to Bobbio, covering the same ground as Augustine

St Matthew's Gospel after the Book of Kells – a famous Celtic Monastery. The same style is found in Bobbio, 8th century.

but with different ideals and enthusiasms. I now had two pilgrimages to unravel. While Augustine and his forty companions, brilliant though they may well have been, made their sedate way through the wild political ferment described by Gregory of Tours, Columban and his twelve disciples were taking their own vivid and lively part in the drama of the pilgrimage. I can now see that Pope Gregory and Brunhilda were both well aware of Columban's 'fast growing religion' in the monasteries at Annegray, Luxeuil and Fontaine with their stern Irish rule. He was winning thousands of ordinary people to come under his influence. Augustine was well advised by Pope Gregory and Brunhilda to keep clear of this Irishman and his companions.

A New Springtime

These two pilgrimages, both aided and abetted by the mysterious intercession of Bishop Martin of Tours as they criss–crossed each other over Europe, are not merely fascinating studies for the scholar to dissect (important though they may be). Here we find ourselves groping for the very roots of our civilization, where so much clear sanctity is mixed up with so much viciousness. We can begin to understand the sadness of our beloved Ireland today, the land of the saints, going through its current ghastly trauma. We watch day by day on our television sets reports of killings, the tragic funerals and blood feuds that seem to be of almost mythical origin. At times it seems as if the killings and the sectarianism are so ingrained that we feel quite helpless to change the situation. But there is a new springtime of the churches stirring, and millions of people of goodwill are sensing it. Many thousands of devout people of

all denominations are gathering together to go on pilgrimage for unity, enjoying the physical experience of travelling together and the mutual conversations as they go, but above all, spending time together in these holy places in silence, praying speak Lord, for I am listening'.

These pilgrimages will change the world, soul by soul, exactly as they did when Gregory the dynamic pope elect of Rome galvanised the whole city and organised all the Christians to go on pilgrimage in procession over the river Tiber to Santa Maria Maggiore, and also began a new springtime of the church: or as when the quiet Augustine and his group set off (rather shyly, I guess) with their cross for Canterbury; or that ball of fire, Columban, who left his beloved Ireland to go with his group on pilgrimage to Luxeuil and Bobbio, all with such good effect. These pilgrimages *work!*

I have discovered that the centre point of all these pilgrimages is not Rome or Canterbury, Bangor or Bobbio, but the rather sad great basilica at Tours where the remains of Bishop Martin lie. I would urge pilgrims to spend time on this sacred spot praying fervently for peace wherever there is unrest or strife.

For me the most beloved spot of all is a stone's throw from Tours, at Marmoutier. There is the cell of Bishop Martin under the great cliffs, cliffs that are dotted with caves where so many hundreds of Celtic and Irish saints lived out their lives, waiting for the spark from heaven to fall. One day I climbed up the steep stairs to the caves guided by a very old nun, and then spent the rest of the day sitting down by Martin's cell, whilst the cocks and hens pecked about in the piles of dung spread over the fields. All seemed deeply moving in the silence.

The Way of the pilgrim to the
Holy Land — after a wood cut
from William Ways.

Informacion for Pylgrymage.
1498

CHAPTER FOUR

Preparations for the Pilgrimage

THE PASSIONATE MAN'S PILGRIMAGE
Supposed to be written by One at the Point of Death
by Sir Walter Ralegh

Give me my scallop-shell of quiet,
My staff of faith to walk upon,
My scrip of joy, immortal diet,
My bottle of salvation,
My gown of glory, hope's true gage,
And thus I'll take my pilgrimage.

And this is my eternal plea
To him that made heaven, earth and sea:
Seeing my flesh must die so soon,
And want a head to dine next noon,
Just at the stroke when my veins start and spread,
Then am I ready, like a palmer fit,
To tread those blest paths which before I writ.

Sir Walter Ralegh (1552–1618) had been put in the tower a number of times, threatened with execution, let out a number of times, but in the end had to face the stroke, and his veins did start and spread. For me his poem says all that can be said about the perfect pilgrimage.

Like Hazlett I have always loved to wander off on my own for a whole day at a time, leaving my cares behind me, to let things happen in my mind, to take in the beauty of the countryside and to meet who I may. But now my wanderings have become a passion, for intimations of a focus to my wanderings have set me on this pilgrimage, on my own, to head for Rome, and then to make my way home to Canterbury.

An important intimation was in the 1960s during the time when I was rector of St Martin's and St Paul's churches in Canterbury. On my free Mondays, with the little dog Mitzi, I would walk for miles following the river Stour which I have loved since I was a child. Sometimes, if the weather was fair I would take my little homemade canoe and paddle up the river. This began my passion to travel from its source to its mouth at Sandwich. The idea blossomed and I made illustrated leaflets of the statutory footpaths so that others might also enjoy the riverside.

I began to meet people who became interested in my ideas. Among them was Mr Nigel Nicholson of Sissinghurst who, with his family, had a love of canoeing on the Stour. When I produced a small book called *Six Walks along the Stour* I told him how I had stumbled on the fact that the footpaths I was walking were those used by Augustine when he made his famous great English Pilgrimage, so graphically recalled by Bede. I went on to say how I would like to write up the route of pilgrimage from Thanet to Canterbury. Nigel quite laconically said that he had just been to Rome and had seen the plaque in St Andrew's Monastery in the Caelian Hills to commemorate the start of Augustine's pilgrimage to England on the orders of Pope Gregory the Great, and why did I not do the whole walk: from Rome? It seems that God leads us sometimes by strange means along fore-ordained paths. Thus began my passion for pilgrimage from Rome which over the intervening years grew and flourished.

I realised that 1997 would be the fourteen hundredth anniversary of Augustine's great pilgrimage and I wanted to write it all down so as to help other pilgrims who might want to celebrate this event by making their own journey. I could visualise many thousands of people setting out from Rome and travelling through that glorious European countryside, on foot perhaps like Augustine, or by coach, train, car or even, for a considerable part of the way, by boat.

Seven years ago I suffered a cerebral infraction or stroke, which left me sometimes very confused, and ultimately with slight deafness. I have since had a number of epileptic fits. Despite these handicaps I was determined to complete my task with God's help and guidance. I received the blessing with laying on of hands from Agnes and Gerald Hooper, the healers at

Kingston near Taunton in Somerset. I was anointed with holy oils and received much help from other healers and many people besides. The day arrived when I was able once again to celebrate the Eucharist with the encouragement of our small country congregation. I began to cycle around the lanes again and walked for miles on my own, bathed in the farm pond every day in the summer and gradually, I praise God, recovered slowly. The idea of the Pilgrimage once again became a real possibility. In short, like Sir Walter Ralegh I had had a brush with death, and if I did die in Rome, like Keats, then I felt it would be rather a good way to go, better anyway than to linger miserably and unfulfilled.

Practical Preparations

You will hear within your own ears a voice behind you saying, This is the way: follow it. (Isaiah 30.21)

It was as if these and other similar words kept coming to me from different directions – not words that were physically heard but a persistent mystical guidance. During my thirteen years as rector of St Martin's church at Canterbury my churchwarden was Col. John Haddon. Together we had become deeply involved in the Unity Movement, lighting a candle weekly on Thursdays, the day when Jesus prayed that all his followers might be as one 'that the world may believe' (John 17.21). Together we had worked especially hard in the weeks of prayer for Christian Unity. Over the years since then I have kept in touch with John and now, when I mentioned the problem I had of finding a sympathetic place where this old Don Quixote could stay in Rome, imagine my surprise when he told me he had recently been appointed as the organiser of a world wide appeal for the Anglican Centre in Rome. This centre had been established in response to Pope John XXIII's Second Vatican Council and had the support of all Anglican archbishops. Imagine, also, my surprise when I discovered that the Anglican Centre was being run by two members of the Society of the Sacred Mission, the same community that had trained me for the priesthood at Kelham.

I immediately wrote to the director, Douglas Brown, and it was soon arranged that I should stay there in October. He even thought he might be able to find a young student to accompany me on my travels home to Canterbury. I then wrote to friends and to some religious communities I knew about the project and asked them all to keep me in their prayers. Knowing they were praying for me was a great support and encouragement.

Pope John XXIII

Setting out with a Blessing

On 18 October 1992, at the main Eucharist in our village church in Merriott, Somerset, our vicar announced to the congregation my plans. I stood up and told them all about my pilgrimage plans, and he blessed me in their midst. That same afternoon my wife and a friend waved me off on the train and I suddenly wondered whether I had been stupid to go, and if I would return or not. I muddled my way through Gatwick Airport with my knapsack on my back and an increasingly heavy suitcase, far too full of books, weighing me down. I felt more and more like Bunyan's Pilgrim weighed down by his sin and guilt. I longed to find somewhere I could buy a folding, wheeled trolley!

At 5 pm the aircraft started to trundle down the runway. It was full of passengers and I thought how incredible it was that so many of us with our bags and baggage would soon be suspended in the air in this great machine. The engine noise increased to a roar and we were away, soaring above the clouds, at first silver, but then tinged with the red of the evening sun. I felt no fear, just exhilaration.

> Whither shall I go then from thy presence
> If I climb up into heaven, thou art there:
> If I go down to hell, thou art there also.
>
> If I take the wings of the morning, and remain
> in the uttermost parts of the sea,
> Even there also shall thy hand lead me.
> (Psalm 139.7–10)

The pilot pointed out the Alps which we could see in the distance through breaks in the clouds. This was where Columban and his companions had wandered about proclaiming the gospel – and there suddenly Lake Geneva and what I felt must be the rivers Rhône and Saône, which had carried Augustine and his companions and would guide me home, snaking away in the distance. In the sunset there was a golden cloud which I gazed at until we began the slow descent towards the thousands of pinbright lights that were Rome.

As pilgrims of old wore a pilgrimage badge to identify themselves, so I now wore mine. I had made two strong cardboard shields, each approximately 12.5 x 14 cms, one to hang around my neck for all to see, the other to give to Douglas Brown at the Anglican Centre. As a boy I had been one of the fifty Scholars of the Chapter of Canterbury Cathedral and so used the school crest as my badge. We touched down, entered the terminal building and were reunited with our luggage.

A Ukranian student living at the Anglican Centre named Serge Sheiko was there to greet me as I emerged from the airport. Very soon I was at the Anglican Centre in the heart of Rome. I was welcomed by Douglas Brown and felt immediately at home, the home of six years in community as a young man and the home of all the vicarage years since.

The Anglican Centre in Rome

The Anglican Centre was founded by one of the members of the Doria family in the 1960s. Pope John XXIII had established the Second Vatican Council in St Peter's on 11 October 1962, which was to usher in a quite new era, particularly for the Unity of all Christians. Archbishop Fisher was the first Christian leader to accept his invitation to send observers to the Council. Not only did the bishops of the whole Anglican community set up a standing representative, such as Douglas Brown today, to encourage the work, but out of this, one of the members of the Doria family offered the top flat of the Palazzo for a centre, and from this beginning the work has gone from strength to strength.

It was a strange experience to be living in a palace, and there were signs of former glory, such as the gaps on the staircase where the stair rods had been. My room in the top flat was very large and there were photographs of Archbishop Michael Ramsey with Pope Paul VI, and Pope John Paul II with Archbishop Runcie. I looked out of my window and it seemed as if the whole of Rome was at my feet. The history of the Palazzo Doria Pamphili is long and goes back to Ancient Rome. The present facade was added in about 1734 when its owners were princes and princesses of the Holy Roman Empire with their retinue of 'gentlemen of the household', artists, musicians and trusted servants. It is still lived in in this style. An inconspicuous little door opens into one of Rome's most famous picture galleries which houses the Velasquez portrait of the Pamphili family Pope, Innocent X. From 1966 to 1990 the centre was generally funded by the Anglican Consultative Council, but budget constraints forced the Council to reduce its funding to about £40,000 a year for the period 1991–1993. After that it will almost certainly be nominal. The bishops have therefore appealed for £1,500,000 to establish an adequate endowment fund and thereby secure the future of the Centre.

As I write this, I now realise how I

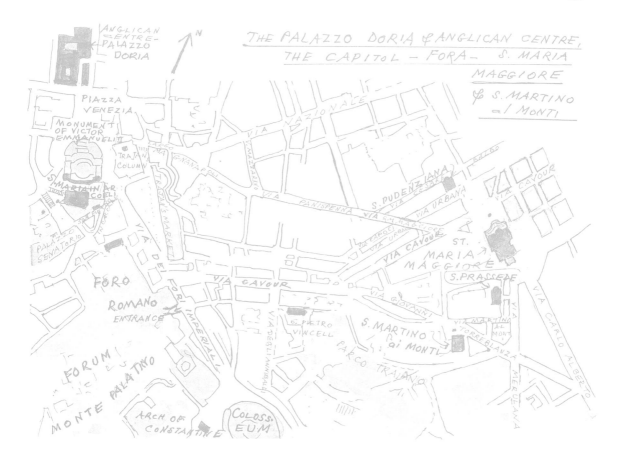

was taking advantage of the remarkable opportunity that had come my way to try and write this book 'In the Footsteps of St Augustine from Rome to Canterbury' ready for the anniversary in 1997 of the first pilgrimage of 597. I could see clearly the wisdom of those who had set up the Anglican Centre in the sixties to help heal the rifts between Christians, and I was determined to do my part.

The scene on coming out of the Palazzo Doria Anglican Centre

CHAPTER FIVE

Exploring Rome

Monday 19 October

I woke on the Monday greatly refreshed. After Matins and breakfast with the group I was ready to go out. October is an excellent time of year to explore Rome. It is warm but rather prone suddenly to pour with rain for about half an hour at a time and then brighten up again. Because of this I carried in my satchel a waterproof cloak, sou-wester and a pair of waterproof trousers. I wore waterproof overshoes. I left the Centre determined however to soak myself, if possible, in Pope Gregory's atmosphere of AD 540–604, and to come to terms with the Emperor Constantine (AD 274–337) as he founded the Western world.

I also wanted to find out any inkling about my mysterious St Martin of Tours. I had with me the excellent *Blue Guide* a very *sine qua non*, which enables one to delve into every corner of the City. I had my own old copy of H.V. Morton's *A Traveller in Rome* which gives vivid glimpses of Rome, and later bought a copy of the large and up to date *The Companion Guide to Rome* by Georgina Masson which is an excellent guide. There was so much to see and do in Rome it was quite bewildering, but now that I am back home I have been able to brood over it all again with these books. Before I began I had determined not to be sidetracked on my pilgrimage by all the remarkable buildings of the Gothic triumphs, the Renaissance wonders of art or the delights of the Rococo graceful ornamentations. I wanted to concentrate on trying to dig down to find every sign of the early Christian Church; and the vestiges of the triumphs of those who had sacrificed themselves in the persecutions in ancient Rome (AD 30–325). I was then determined to find the quite different triumphs of the establishment of Christianity by the Emperor Constantine and the wonders of ancient pagan and Christian Rome. I wanted to see the signs of the numerous attacks on the city by Alaric of the Visigoths of 452 Attila with his host of Franks, Huns and Vandals, and others like Totila the Goth who took the city in AD 546, and to chart the city's ups and downs. All of this I had read about in Morton's book. The Rome in which Gregory was born and grew up was a sad place indeed, as over the years his family had suffered at all these foreign hands. I could quite see how he was determined to build a new world based on the most rigid monastic foundations.

So at last I walked down the long steps of the Palazzo Doria Pamphili, I was out on the pavement and it all looked rather like Piccadilly. The crowds were rushing to and fro. There were the ubiquitous yellow taxis, the crowded orange buses, but above all the scooters, some with two people on them and no helmets, dashing about regardless of left or right, while the dark blue suited policemen with their white topees waved their arms about. Straight in front of me was the blazing white Vittorio Emmanuele Monument, which was sometimes to be too powerful a landmark during my week. It was built to commemorate Italy's first king, Vittorio Emmanuele II in 1911 in honour of the unification of Italy, and was later used to house the tomb of the Unknown Warrior, as I could see from the soldiers standing on guard. Within the first few pages of my childhood history books, there was always a picture of St Gregory and St Augustine talking to the fairhaired Anglo-Saxon boys in their chains who were waiting to be sold as slaves in the Forum. So I set off straightaway for the Forum as I knew it was near the Capitol, the smallest but most famous of the Seven Hills of Rome. I walked to the right of the Vittorio Emanuelle Monument and was immediately faced by two steep

The CORDONATA & CASTOR & POLLUX   Michaelangelos steps to the capitol.

One of the heavenly twins

flights of steps. I climbed the one hundred and twenty steps of that on the left, which was built in 1348 as a thank-offering for the end of the black death. Looking down, the view was remarkable, for I could see my first sight of the great Forum of Trajan, where the massive market centred, crowned by the Emperor Trajan's famous monument. I went on into the great church called the Santa Maria in Aracoeli (St Mary of the Heavens), the first of the many Roman churches I was to go into. This vast, forbidding, gloomy church dates from the sixth century and was already known as 'old' in 574. I knew that Gregory would have known it, with its great columns. The church occupies the site of the Roman Citadel, the hub of Ancient Rome, and rose over the ruins of a temple dedicated to Juno, the pagan mother-goddess, so it was easily consecrated to the Christian Blessed Virgin Mary. Its great columns once graced classical temples and its pavement and monuments gleamed

with fragments of marble from the ancient ruins. The spot is where the Emperor Augustus (27 BC–AD 14) in a vision, saw an altar raised on high, and two voices called from heaven: 'This is the Virgin who will receive in her womb the Saviour of the world – this is the altar of the Son of God'.

Legend or no, as I wandered round in the church I ignored as often as I could the Renaissance pictures, perhaps to my cost, but tried to visualise these great bare barracks with perhaps ikons here and there and candles, as Gregory and Augustine and his monks would have known it as they made their 'stations' of thanks to the Mother of God. I did, however, see the little 'Santo Bambino', the Christ-child supposed to have been carved out of one of the olive trees from the Garden of Gethsemane. I saw, too, for the first time, a reminder of the Emperor Constantine and his family, whose presence would dog my steps in Rome. Here is the altar of St Helena, Constantine's mother, who herself made such a great impression on the Christianising of the Empire, and who by tradition is said to have found the wood of the cross on which Jesus died. There is a small porphyry urn there said to contain her remains.

Like the noble Duke of York, I then went to the bottom of the steps and walked up the much easier steps to the right called the cordonata. I had to stop to take a photograph of the two large stone statues of nude men with swan-like caps on their heads, so aggressively masculine, each with a great half rampant horse beside him, guarding the pale orange Senator's Palace, the top which I could see in the very centre of the Capitol. These are the statues of Castor and

Pollux, the Dioscuri, the heavenly twins, born of the secret copulation of the great god Jupiter and Leda the swan. They were beloved in Ancient Rome and were said to have assisted the Romans at the battle of Lake Regillus. Three columns still stand as part of their temple in the Forum which I was to see later. While climbing up these steps I felt there was something majestic about them, and afterwards I discovered that these steps had been designed by none other than Michelangelo, whose triumphal pictures and designs dominate so much of Renaissance Rome (1475–1564). At the top there is another inspiring view over the city. It was necessary to stop to get my breath, which gave me the chance to try and pick out the city sights below me.

Walking over the Piazza, or square, over all Michelangelo's designs, I passed on the left of the church of Santa Maria in Aracoeli and the most famous Capitoline Museum, which I guess could fascinate and keep anyone occupied for hours, and on the right the great Palazza de Conservatori with its museum, and straight in front the Senator's Palace, originally designed by Michelangelo but completed later by others, right on the site of the ancient Roman Tabularium or Record Office, dating from 78BC. As I walked over the Piazza I was walking over the very site of the great golden temples of Jupiter and Juno. The Jupiter altar must have been a sight for the gods to behold, as the oxen were sacrificed, one after the other, by the butchering priests. The aroma of roast beef suffusing the area must sometimes have been rather tantalising. During the sacrifices all the gifts and jewels would have been piled up, only, sadly, to be grabbed by later invaders. The old Romans were fascinat-

ing people. It seems they loved killing and bloodshed. They loved especially free gifts and all sport and laughed at other people's discomfiture, yet they loved their home rituals, and where indeed would our Christmas rituals be, without the influence of the Romans and their worship of Saturn and his jolly temple in the Forum.

One of the joys of being alone on the loose like this was that I was able to wander at will. It seemed as if I was being led past the great light orange coloured Senator's Palace and past a fountain. I saw people staring intently towards a tall tower and in the far distance a line of the kind of trees that were to become so familiar, and right in front of me as I stood at a railing, what looked like the top of a massive white stone monument. I had arrived, for there was the great triumphal arch of the Emperor Septimius Severus and his wife. Born in Africa in AD 146 Severus was a ruthless and successful ruler, winning campaigns in the East, in Byzantium and who then came to Britain in AD 208, crushed the rebellion and repaired and enlarged Hadrian's Wall. He died, of all places, in York in AD 211, with his concern unfulfilled for Britain.

As I gazed out I realised I had arrived, and like St Paul 'I must see Rome'. As I stood on the Capitol and looked past Severus' Arch I could see the piles of stones of the great Forum. There was so much to see and take in I thought I should never be able to sort it all out on my own, but as I looked at the whole scene I had a Gregorian revelation. For there in the far distance was the Colosseum and behind it to the right St Gregory's own church and his monastery on the Caelian Hill where he had been so

The Arch of Septimius Severus

preoccupied with thoughts of Britain. There too, Constantine's (AD 306–337) great white arch where he too had been so full of Britain as he set off to conquer the world for Christ. There was the forum and remains of the basilica of Julius Caesar (102–44 BC) who also played so great a part in Britain's history with his 'veni – vidi – vici'. I was reminded of yet another British connection when I saw the temple of Vespasian (Emperor AD 69–79) and thought of his successors Hadrian (Emperor AD 117–138) and Aurelian (Emperor AD 270–275) who out of their care for Britain caused their great walls to be built, the same walls we still see today in the north of our island. To cap it all, not far from Gregory's own monastery I saw the remains of the Emperor Claudius (Emperor AD 41–52) the

stutterer, who deified himself. He came to Britain in person and conquered it completely, landing with his elephants at the castle at Richborough in Kent, which I know so well.

I now see that all these great men who had made the Roman Empire had the British itch. I can see how Gregory, growing up as he did in highly privileged surroundings, going to school and living in the city, must also have felt Britain calling him with its magic and mystery. In fact, he even set off himself to conquer it for Christ. John his deacon describes how Gregory, together with some companions, started off for Britain. He had gone three days journey before the people at Rome found he had gone, clamoured for him to be their pope and sent messengers after him. The story goes that it was midday and Gregory and his group were resting. A 'locusta' (locust) settled on Gregory's book as he was reading, which caused him to say 'that means *loco sta*, stay in this place'. Soon after this the messengers arrived from Rome imploring him to return with them. Clearly Gregory, like so many old Romans, had the British itch.

After a long time brooding over it all with great excitement I at last turned my eyes towards the left and could see a strange series of vivid orange buildings including a chapel. This is called St Peter in the Prison. It was built in 387 BC as a cistern and later served as a prison where the enemies of Rome were thrown, often to die of starvation or be brutally killed. Legend has it that Nero (Emperor AD 54–68) had St Peter kept there until his public death. The whole area is even more grim as on the way down from the campidoglio on the right hand side is the Tarpeian Rock from where, in ancient times, people guilty of treason were hurled to their death. Tarpeia was a Vestal Virgin who betrayed the city to the Sabine soldiers, then beseiging Rome, on condition that they gave her their golden bracelets from their left hands. In disgust they flung their shields on her and left her body at the base of the rock.

As I walked on down the Via del Foro Romano towards Trajan's column, where so many conquering rulers and emperors had wound their way up the Via Sacra to the Capitol temples, I could not but help remember how the Emperor Claudius came up here with his legions in triumphant procession after conquering Britain. His prisoners of war included the British king Caractacus, his wife and daughter. Caractacus and his fellow prisoners were terrified and humiliated by the jeers and catcalls of the watching crowds and some of them pleaded for mercy. On reaching the dais before the emperor Caractacus made a very brave speech. He pointed out that no one would ever remember either his downfall or the emperor's triumph if he were to be executed. He argued that to spare him would be an everlasting token of Claudius' mercy and greatness. Claudius was so impressed he released him, his wife and brothers. Many speeches were made in the Senate hailing the encounter as equal in glory to any previous Roman general's behaviour to captured royalty. This story was told by Tacitus (AD 54–120) in *Tacitus on Imperial Rome*.

Gregory would have known his Tacitus well and loved this story of Britons. This thought cheered me greatly as I crossed the Via dei Fori Imperiali and found Trajan's Column and the markets of Trajan's forum. The Via dei Fori Imperiali is a splendid highway 850 metres long and 30 metres wide which runs the length of the old Roman Fora and was opened in October 1933 after having been systematically cleared since 1925. It is lined with trees and flower gardens and is a pleasant thoroughfare full of ancient history. At this point I felt it was time for luncheon and a siesta so I walked back to the Anglican Centre at the Palazzo Doria Pamphili. I passed a man sitting in an empty bus with the sign INFORMAZIONE on it, a welcome sign for any pilgrim.

A word on Roman buses – to travel by bus you need a ticket and the bus ticket system in Rome is an experience to be savoured. There are rules which everyone crowding on and off the buses seemed to ignore completely, which did not help an old deaf Englishman like me, but everyone was so willing to help that bus journeys were an enjoyable experience.

I was glad to get back to the Anglican Centre after this first experience of Rome, and I felt exhilarated by it all. After an excellent lunch I was advised to take my time at my siesta and sleep, as the midday siesta is universal in the warm seasons of the year, and shops are often open later into the evenings to take account of it. At mealtimes there was always, in the centre of the table, a splendid china bowl of luscious bright large oranges, grapes, shiny red apples and passion fruit. As I sat later in the library before I slept I picked up a lovely book about the catacombs and basilicas of the early Christians in Rome. On opening it I found a picture which might have been of our modern fruit bowl. The painting was by an unknown artist working in the catacombs at the time when the early Christians were celebrating their love feasts. I made a rough sketch of these fruit bowls

After a copy of S. Sebastian's fresco in catacomb

as they made me think of the loveliness and happiness of those early worshippers as they joyfully knew that the Lord Jesus would receive their spirits to everlasting life whatever persecutions they might suffer. I went to bed and slept soundly and woke refreshed. After tea I went back to Trajan's column and the walls of his forum.

Trajan's Column

I was quite staggered by the size of everything and the intricacy of the carving on the column depicting legionaries marching busily round and round, spiralling to the top. The column is some 30 metres high and in 1588 a statue of St Peter was placed on top of it to celebrate Trajan's reputedly compassionate attitude to Christians. Pliny, one of his Governors, had written and asked him if he should put Christians to death for their faith. Trajan made no hard and fast rule in his answer, as some emperors such as Nero had done. The Emperor Trajan (Emperor AD 98–117) was the most robust and soldierly of all and beloved by his troops everywhere, but he could be very ruthless. On many occasions he simply massacred by the thousand those who opposed him. It is recorded that on one of his Triumphs, after the Dacian War for instance, ten thousand gladiators and eleven thousand beasts were killed over a four month period of 'games'. In his book *A Traveller in Rome*, H.V. Morton gives an account of a story which has been passed down from one generation to another that Gregory the Great:

> . . . touched by Trajan's compassion for the poor and widows, asked God to open the gates of the Christian heaven to this good and compassionate pagan, and that God, not too willingly, answered Gregory's prayer. (pp. 50–51)

Trajan's ashes are in a golden urn at the bottom of the column. There is a spiral stair inside with 185 steps, while outside the 2,500 figures wind round and up to the top. There are depicted all the possible kinds of tough masculine legionaries who had been trained, bullied, drilled, and generally licked into shape by Trajan

'I was quite staggered by the size of everything' . . . Trajan's column

and his captains to make up a legion on one of Trajan's Triumphs, coming home from the Dacian Wars.

Here the cavalry and the navy, engineers and bridge builders, doctors, surgeons and legionaries with their shields are all fixed forever in stone. On the way up to the Capitol, himself borne up aloft wearing his red and gold toga one can imagine the crowds cheering and the legionaries marching and perhaps making plans amongst themselves for the games and general wantonness that would follow the formal procession.

Amazed by the grandeur and the thoughts that had been triggered by the

Intricacy of the carving on Trajan's column

sight of this great column I nearly missed the fact that all around this place was the last and greatest of the Fora in Rome the great walls around about represented Rome's hypermarket of the time, soaring up behind the Quirinal hill, another of Rome's seven hills. It must have been a remarkable place of three storeys in which every conceivable kind of produce was sold. I longed to find the slave market where Gregory saw the fair haired Angles waiting to be sold, but I never could, and no one seemed to be able to tell me where it was. Nevertheless it was good while I was in this great forum to brood over slavery as the Romans and Gregory saw it. In the first place slavery in Rome was never the degrading and brutal institution of the seventeenth and eighteenth centuries when slaves had no rights. If a master killed a slave the master had to appear before a court of justice. If he ill-treated his slave it was a penal offence. In the great mansions or large households where slaves, male and female, lived quite happily as a family, it was sometimes possible for a rite of manu-mission to take place so that the slave was given his or her freedom. It must have been a great occasion. The master turned the slave round with the words '*liber esto*' (be free), in the presence of a magistrate, who struck the slave with his rod. The master then gave the slave a letter and a hat of liberty, often of his master's colours. About this time, too, a new style of giving of full freedom was taking place so that properly ordained clerics could by mere expression of will, liberate their slaves. I could now understand why Gregory, full of his vision of converting Britain for Christ, was so keen to find cultured young men among the British slaves who could be given their freedom and be trained for the religious life under his guidance and patronage.

Back at the Anglican Centre I relaxed in the excellent library, dipping in it and working out a few things that in my naïvety muddled me. In the first place what was a forum? The original forum was a marshy valley lying between the Capitoline, which I had already visited, and the Palatine hills. Over the years it had become the very centre of every kind of the city's life. Religious ceremonies and sacrifices were held there, as well as the Triumphs which welcomed home victorious emperors, and elections and the broadcasting of important news. In short the centre of the community, where everything could be seen openly. As the city grew, other fora developed.

Then I began to wonder what was the difference between a basilica and a church? The word basilica is derived from the feminine of the Greek adjective *basilikos*, meaning royal. In ancient Rome a basilica was simply a large building or two near the Forum, where people could meet indoors. As the city developed these basilicas became larger and larger and were erected with huge columns to support them. It is quite easy to see how when Constantine Christianised Rome,

Rough sketch of the Nave of the Basilica of old St. Peters as it was in the 16th century.

many of these basilicas were simply converted into religious buildings or churches. It was the end of my first day and, after reading H.V. Morton's vivid description of the triumphal arches of Rome (p. 59), I dozed off into a long and easy sleep. It had been a good day.

Tuesday 20 October

The Forum

After Matins with the community I was ready to start exploring the rest of the Roman Forum, and in the afternoon I planned to walk to the Colosseum, which seems to dominate the mind of every visitor to Rome, because of its powerful influence. I made for the Via dei Fori Imperiali again and walked over the ancient Fora of Rome, as yesterday, until I found an entrance, opposite the Via Cavour, where I asked: 'Quanto?' (how much). To my surprise the girl asked if I was English, and when I said: 'si', she gave me a ticket, free.

The moment I went in I realised I should have gone with an English guide. I had to spend so much time later trying to piece the experience together. I wandered up a footpath on to a grassy mound in the rain and realised I was looking down, on the Stadium, a green enclosure with low ruins on either side. In fact I was standing on the Palatine Hill, another of the seven hills of Rome, and according to tradition, the first to be occupied and the nucleus of the city. This stadium was the venue for private races and athletic contests and may, at some time have been a private garden for the enjoyment of the emperors and privileged members of their families. I found it hard to imagine how the emperors and their reti-

nues lived in such palatial style up here, especially Septimius Severus who busied himself by enlarging it, while they looked over the busy city below. In the pouring rain and without my English guide I began to feel like poor Arthur Hugh Clough (1819–1861) who wrote:

> Rome disappoints me much . . . This, however, perhaps is the weather, which truly is horrid. Rubbishy seems the word that most exactly would suit it. Would to Heaven the old Goths had made a clean sweep of it.

There was nobody around until at last I saw an elderly couple looking dejected. I tried my Italian again: 'Forum, si?' 'Ooh aye, along there,' said the old chap, and there it was. I could see the Septimius Severus Arch and above it the Capitol I had seen the day before, and there stood the mass of ruins that Gregory had known so well and loved, and which had shaped not only his vision but that of the rather more timid Augustine, his personal friend. I was reminded of my time at Ligugé near Poitiers, studying where St Martin had lived, in the monastery of the Benedictine community there. I used to sit sketching and was able to watch every afternoon how the monks went out for their stately country walks and talked together. Here and now I could imagine, rain or no rain, how Gregory and Augustine and his community (especially the young) could well from time to time have come here for their afternoon walks.

As I came down into the Forum itself it stopped raining. I took off my waterproofs, and the gentle blue sky with pleasant white clouds seemed to change the whole scene and I could begin to give my imagination full rein. I was standing on the Via Sacra, the Sacred Way, where all

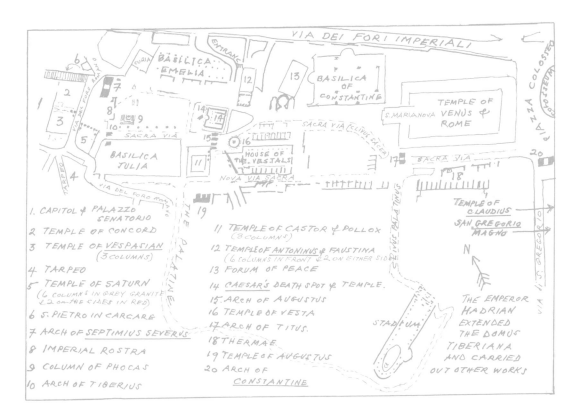

1. CAPITOL & PALAZZO SENATORIO
2. TEMPLE OF CONCORD
3. TEMPLE OF VESPASIAN (3 COLUMNS)
4. TARPEO
5. TEMPLE OF SATURN (6 COLUMNS IN GREY GRANITE & 2 ON THE SIDES IN RED)
6. S. PIETRO IN CARCARE
7. ARCH OF SEPTIMIUS SEVERUS
8. IMPERIAL ROSTRA
9. COLUMN OF PHOCAS
10. ARCH OF TIBERIUS
11. TEMPLE OF CASTOR & POLLOX (3 COLUMNS)
12. TEMPLE OF ANTONINUS & FAUSTINA (6 COLUMNS IN FRONT & 2 ON EITHER SIDE)
13. FORUM OF PEACE
14. CAESAR'S DEATH SPOT & TEMPLE.
15. ARCH OF AUGUSTUS
16. TEMPLE OF VESTA
17. ARCH OF TITUS.
18. THERMAE.
19. TEMPLE OF AUGUSTUS
20. ARCH OF CONSTANTINE

THE EMPEROR HADRIAN EXTENDED THE DOMUS TIBERIANA AND CARRIED OUT OTHER WORKS

these great processions and triumphs brought the emperors and generals from the east, south, west and the north. I could imagine their marching, colour, and music, just as I could remember those great State processions I had seen, from Buckingham Palace up the Mall, along the Strand to Fleet Street, to meet the Lord Mayor and go on to St Paul's Cathedral.

So I wandered with the aid of my guide book. Everyone can find the three columns of the temple of the Dioscuri Castor and Pollux, and I was again amazed by the size of their statues. They had to have their own temple because of their Intercessary power with the gods in times of trouble in Rome, and they were much loved and honoured by everyone. Next to this was the Basilica of Julius, started by Caesar himself and finished by

Augustus. It was near here that Mark Anthony made his oration after Caesar's assassination (15 March 44 BC) before the sorrowing and furious Roman populace who had previously hailed and celebrated Caesar's four Triumphs along this very Sacra Via. Next door was the temple of Saturn. Saturn was the mythical figure who taught his people the art of husbandry. I could visualise the joy of the happy festivities here. Gregory was instrumental in Christianising these rejoicings into our Christmas festivities when 'the Word was made flesh' (John 1.14). Then the slave and his master changed places, the houses were decked, as ours are today, with greenery and flowers and feasting was the order of the day. The temple of Saturn must have been a magnificent building. It is said that the foundation of the temple was built in 497 BC though there were a number of reconstructions.

As I wandered around these temples I could not help looking at the desolation of it all. It was as if there had been some divine intervention. For in the days of Nero the beginning of a strange new Christian sect was emerging, so strict that not one of them would take even the smallest part in the pleasant sacrifices; the old rituals and the new faith were clearly on a collision course. So I moved on next door to the temple of Vespasian, no legendary person but a flesh and blood man, a plain blunt soldier who lived out a fine full strong life, with a great sense of coarse humour. In his last moments he is said to have said: 'Methinks I am becoming a god'.

Many of these happy yet sad temple worshippers visualised the Emperor going to heaven in glory. But for those of the new Christian faith there was no nostalgic way about it, it was personal faith straight from the heart with a living hero, Jesus.

Turning my back on the three beautiful Corinthian columns of Vespasian and the temple of Concordia, I came face to face again with the Arch of Septimius Severus. As I stood beside it I again thought of his dying there in agony in York, determined to keep Britain as part of the Empire, with its fledgling secret Christianity beginning to take-off. Next door to it is the Rostra Caesar, the pulpit where orators would deliver their speeches and harangues. The rostra were originally constructed like the prows of war vessels, presumably to allow for good acoustics for the great assemblies. It was at this very Rostra where Mark Anthony made his speech after Caesar's assassination. There is the curia, the

austere red brick building which was built in the reign of the emperor Diocletian (Emperor AD 284–305), though the original curia is reputedly to have been built by Romulus, the founder of Rome. The curia is the building where the senate met, each member in his purple bordered robes with his ivory wand in his hand, and seated on his curule chair. In the far distance was the golden statue of the Goddess of Victory, before which they all, at every session, offered wine and incense. It was good to stand there and think for a moment, how, after the pronouncement of the ratification of the Council of Nicaea in AD 325 the Emperor Constantine had virtually begun the dismantling of the pagan religions and rites and dismissing their priests and priestesses. It was no easy task, and it was not until 375 that Valentinian's son ordered the statue of Victory to be removed. There was war in the end and the statue was returned in 392, but then finally destroyed.

I stood at the remains of Caesar's temple near the site of Mark Anthony's famous oration, and what sympathy I felt for this great man who had such an influence on the whole world, and yet was so pathetic at his end. At the age of fifty eight, riddled with bad health and suffering frequent epileptic fits which must have been humiliating, he became forgetful and bad tempered, looked fatigued and overworked, yet underneath it all his passion was unabated not only for 'the West' but especially Britain, and kept his day by day personal account of it all.

There is the Temple of the Vestals and near it their own grand house. Right in the centre of Rome's essentially masculine centre, where it seemed women could only appear on suffrance, here it was. Not only were they most cultured and cherished women but they were priestesses, just as important as male priests. I mused on our present day quarrels about 'women priests' and thought that if our new ministry is not to be clouded by priestcraft, might we not rejoice like our early Christian forefathers and speak of our 'ministers' as 'presbyters' and 'elders' and not 'priests' and 'priestesses'. The six virgin pagan priestesses of Rome guarded the holy fire in the domed Temple of Vesta. In primitive days when fire was very precious and difficult to light it had been the job of a group of women to ensure the fire was kept alight day and night. In Roman times these six women kept the holy fire alight and people, seeing the wispy smoke rising, knew that all was well with Rome. The Virgin's length of time in the temple was thirty years after which she was free to marry. They had many privileges, such as at the games and at feasts, and always dressed in white robes. When sacrificing, these were bordered with purple and fastened with a brooch on their breast. They were very well off as they were given large dowries by the state. They lived in style and people had to make way for their carriages when they drove out. If, however, they broke their oath of thirty years virginity they were liable to be put to death by entombment.

By now I was ready for a break and to go back to the Anglican Centre for luncheon and for the regulation siesta. On my way I found myself opposite the most remarkable building, the Temple of Antoninus and Faustina, dedicted by the senate in AD 141 to the memory of Empress Faustina and later to her husband Antoninus. Faustina was a curious woman and died young, but Antoninus (Emperor AD 138–161), Hadrian's adopted son, was a remarkably successful Emperor who ushered in a reign of comparative peace because of his compassionate, fair and equitable rule. I stopped and gazed at the soaring Corinthian columns, six in front and two on either side, at the entrance to the Forum and thought what a splendid temple it must have been. As a most compassionate Emperor Antoninus extended to the Christians the strong hand of his protection throughout the Empire. He was also responsible for extending the northern British defences started by his adopted father Hadrian by building the Antoninus Wall which can still be seen today in Scotland. When asked by the tribune of the night watch for the password he said 'Aequanimitas', 'peacefulness'. As I left the mouldering stones of old Rome I felt moved to use this word as a prayer for I felt that St Gregory and St Augustine would influence us and their monks would encourage us.

The Colosseum

After the siesta I set out again along the Via dei Fori Imperiali to find the Colosseum. Even from far away it looked like a colossus. I went past the Forum entrance I had entered that morning, and near the roundabout were some of the pillars of the Temple of Venus and Rome, which had been built by the Emperor Hadrian. It was dedicated to Venus, the mythical mother of Aeneas, and it remained there in use as late as AD 391, long after the last pagan temple had been officially suppressed, so it must have been a centre of gentle, harmless and loving worship. I stood there, among all the figurines for sale, looking up at the great Colosseum. I could easily imagine the excitement at the sport, the ghoulish amusement and bloodthirsty shouts and cries of pain as the fifty thousand spectators watched the entertainments in the arena. It is a remarkable building, about half a kilometre in circumference, 188 metres long by 156 metres wide, 57 metres high and built of stone. It is built on top of an old lake, the idea of the Emperor Vespasian in AD 70, started by his son Titus and completed by Domitian (Emperor AD 81-96). The crowds were able to be seated and could get in and out of the building with ease. I am no architect and the extraordinary rows of arches and columns one upon the other bewilder me, Doric on the lower storey, Ionic on the middle and Corinthian on the top, with slender Corinthian columns on the fourth storey.

The only thing to do was to climb up inside and let the whole magnificent, grotesque scene speak for itself. In his book *A Traveller in Rome* H.V. Morton's de-

The Colosseum and the figurines for sale

'A great black cross commemorated all who suffered martyrdom in the Colosseum'

scription of events held here is splendid. The spectators would all be wearing their white or coloured togas. There were the gruesome gladiatorial fights to the death. The inaugural festival lasted for one hundred days and many gladiators were killed. Gladiators were professional combatants who fought to the death for cash. They were the personal bodyguards of the wealthy and politically powerful. Some of the most valuable ones were the Britons with their chariots. There were gladiatorial schools where they trained to fight, some as short swordsmen with helmet, shield, and armour, some unarmed except for a net and trident. Five thousand wild beasts were trained by the bestiarii, wild animal fighters, to endure their sufferings for longer than they would normally be able. In his *Confessions*, St Augustine of Hippo (AD 354–430), says the whole thing must have been repulsive to watch, and the great shows were put on two or three times a year. The Roman populace must have been furious when, time after time, those of whatever rank from senator to slave who had accepted Christianity, stood there mildly in their tunics, left their weapons on the ground and looked piously towards heaven as they awaited their fate. Real spoil-sports! Among those brought here to suffer was old Bishop St Ignatius of Antioch (died c. AD 110). I came across a great black cross which commemorates all who suffered martyrdom here. So I sat and remembered Bishop Ignatius, who was writing at the time of the Emperor Trajan. In one of his epistles he said he was a Roman citizen and just been sentenced to death, and was being sent, in charge of a band of soldiers to fight the beasts in the amphitheatre:

> I bid all men know that of my own free will I die for God, unless you should hinder me . . . Let me be given to the wild beasts that I may be found the pure bread of Christ. Entice the wild beasts that they may become my sepulchre . . . come fire and cross and grappling with wild beasts, wrenching of bones, hacking of limbs, crushings of my whole body: only be it mine to attain to Jesus Christ.

I went away and joined the bustle of the cabbies outside. Gregory, born and brought up as he was only half a mile away, must have felt the power of personal sacrifice ingrained in his mind.

Arch of Constantine

I crossed over the road by the cabs and there was the Emperor Constantine's great arch. If the Christians in the Roman Colosseum had by their passive conquests virtually won the day for Christianity, it was Constantine who personally changed the whole Roman West, established the Christian Nicene creed as its formula, and eventually on his death bed was baptized himself. As I walked around in the next few days I could see that time and time again it was not Caesar this and Caesar that. Everywhere it was Constantine, Constantine, for this great man, on his own it seemed to me, had shaped our modern European culture; and it was the thought of him that so strongly influenced Gregory. So by his arch I took a photograph and then sat and brooded. In the first place I thought it was rather splendid until I realised it had been made of fragments disinterred before, and architectural people seem to think it is rather poor compared to others in the Forum. But I was deeply moved as I could walk underneath it and realise that this arch was erected in AD 315 by the Senate,

The Arch of Constantine

designed for Constantine to make his Triumph after his victory against his fellow Caesar, Maxentius at the Milvian Bridge. What thoughts must have been his as he was led through this arch, the crowds and his legionaries cheering him on his way.

Constantine was born in AD 288 during the height of the persecution of the Christians. He was the illegitimate son of the Emperor Constantius, and his mother Flavia Helena, who was described by St Ambrose as an inn-keeper, later became none other than St Helena. At the age of eighteen years he had had many adventures and galloped across Europe to find his father, who was dying at York. The legions acclaimed him as Caesar and he set off to conquer Rome, the legions throughout Gaul gathering behind him. (One day when I was in York, in the museum, I saw and loved the great fine statue of him as a young man – so vigorous and like a sort of president of an Oxford or Cambridge University boat club. How strange it is to think how he had set off from York, in all probability to Canterbury on his way via Richborough.) His army met that of the pagan co-emperor Maxentius at the battle of the Milvian Bridge, near Rome, and in the middle of the fight:

> . . . he was praying, and God sent him a miraculous sign. It was afternoon, and the sun was sinking on the horizon, when he saw, in the heavens above the sun, a luminous cross with this inscription attached, TOUTW NIKA (in Greek, 'in this sign, conquer').

As conquerer, he accepted Christianity in a general kind of way, though he was not baptized until his death bed, but the fiercest of the persecutions and the bloodshed was over. Those who had accepted

Constantine the Great
AD 288–337

Christ's way had won a great victory; freedom to read openly the gospels and epistles, freedom to meet together in groups with 'Jesus in the midst' (Luke 24.36), and to share the broken bread and the cup. These things were signs of the victory. Those martyrs who had looked up to heaven through their searing pain had not done so in vain as the Church's ways became the 'ways of gentleness and all her paths are peace' (Sir C. Spring-Rice).

In AD 316 permission was given for the emancipation of slaves to take place in churches. In AD 319 private sacrifices and magic were prohibited, in AD 321 Sundays everywhere were to be called a holiday, and in AD 324 Constantine stigmatized the persecutions and accepted everywhere the sign of the Cross publicly, praying for all his subjects to be Christians, though he compelled none. He ordered the building of some magnificent churches and basilicas everywhere and established a complete new city, dedicated to Christ, at Constantinople, or 'New Rome' where he was to live, and built the magnificent cathedral dedicated to the Holy Wisdom, St Sophia. Finally, in order to make quite clear that the Christianity he had ushered in had no half measures and room for disagreement he, at his own expense, called all the bishops or their representatives to meet at a town called Nicaea, near Constantine's residence in Constantinople, some three hundred and eighteen in number, on 19 June AD 325. The great characters who assembled there, some disfigured by the persecutions, ranged from the simple shepherd Spyridion, to Athanasius the deacon, but above all Constantine himself presided over it all personally. 'At a sign . . . the whole assembly rose', and then for the first time set their amazed gaze on Constantine the Conqueror, the August, the Great. There was a brightness in his look and mingled expression of fierceness and gentleness in his lion-like eyes. His hair was long, crowned with the imperial diadem of pearls. His purple and scarlet robe blazed with precious stones and gold embroidery. After his welcoming address he left the bishops to their own devices but pretty clear in their minds that they must agree in the end. There were disagreements indeed, especially, as according to legend St Nicholas punched the presbyter Arius on the jaw. Anyway, out of it all came what we say every time we keep high Eucharist, the Nicene Creed. It was Eastertide in the year AD 337 when Constantine died after having been baptized.

This Arch of Constantine is a good place to brood. Walk up and down under it and let the Spirit move us in our pilgrimage, to say nothing of asking shades of Gregory and Augustine to aid us on our way. It was a natural idea as I walked home to reflect on the great shell of the Colosseum with its stark cross, and to remember the powerful dynamic faith of our Nicene Creed.

Arch of Titus

I then found the Arch of Titus. The Emperor Titus was the son of Vespasian, and captured Jerusalem on 8 September AD 70 when, as the arch depicts, the spoils of the devastated Temple, never to be recovered, included the altar of Solomon's Temple adorned with trumpets, and the seven branched golden candlestick. The arch, though battered and recovered, may make many devout Jewish people shudder, but it is a place to sit quietly and think of Jesus our Master and His 'prophecies' about the Jerusalem that he had loved so much. May we all, Christians and Jews together be led to a new unity through the Spirit, not only with our Jewish and Palestinian friends, but to the kind of worship that all can share without giving vent to anger about those things that are different in our faiths.

Arch of Titus

The Bascilica of St Clement

Standing by Titus' arch I am afraid I missed realising that the pile of stones I passed was the remains of Constantine's huge basilica, which of course had to be 'the largest' monument in the Forum! I wandered again round Constantine's arch, took another look at the Colosseum, slowly, and then with my *Blue Guide* made my way along the Via di S Giovanni in Laterano to one of the most interesting churches in Rome architecturally, the basilica of St Clement . I was welcomed into the great basilica (and there is no other word for it but 'great') by a very busy, stout, Irish nun only too ready to take my 2,000 lire, and I was on my own. There are really three churches here, one on top of the other. The first, one of the original Christian places of worship. I vaguely recalled with some excitement how the first Christians, who had no churches or cathedrals as we have, met secretly, often underground, in house groups such as those we can read of in St Paul's farewell to the elders of Ephesus (Acts 20.17–38). But it was not until I came to Rome that I understood that these house churches were often great mansions involving large numbers of families, with retainers and slaves galore, and that if the senator and his wife accepted Christianity, many of their 'family' accepted it with them.

The basilica of St Clement had a titulus, one of the seven pastoral areas divided up under Pope Fabian, which began to operate in the first or second century. This mansion belonged to a man called Clement, who was possibly a relation of the consul-martyr Titus Flavius Clemens. The exciting building is now a mixture of medieval and eighteenth century baroque style and I found it rather disap-

pointing, but it seems more than just conjecture that St Clement, (Clement I), was the third Pope of Rome and was banished to the mines by Trajan. He certainly had a great pastoral care for the struggling Christians he knew of, and in his epistle to the Corinthians is written:

> To these men of holy conversation we must add a goodly company of elect souls who gathered round them, and who when by reason of jealousy they were subjected to countless indignities and torture, stood forth as a noble example among us. It was by reason of jealousy that women were persecuted, and subjected under the guise of Danaids and Dirces, to dreadful and unholy violence, until they won the goal for which their faith had struggled.

Archaeologically this is one of the most interesting churches in Rome and it is cared for by the Dominican community. Because of its complicated structure I think it would be better to have the help of a guide, though I wandered about it by myself and probably missed much of it. It seems as if the ground floor rooms were those of the first century mansion of Pope Clement I, and they were used as a house church while the persecutions were raging. On top of that, the Lower Church was built by Pope Siricius (Pope AD 384–399) and has a wide nave, obstructed now by the foundation piers of the upper church. Gregory and Augustine would certainly have been able to wander about in it as it was. The Upper Church was built in AD 1108 by Pope Paschal II.

It is possible to descend into the very fourth century church and see the frescos, copied from the 1857 archaeological discoveries, now to be seen with subdued light. Georgina Masson in her *Companion Guide to Rome* goes into it all in detail and I did as she said and went down stairs to the Mithraic temple. Mithraism it seems to me must have been a very manly religion, with initiations taking place in a rocky cave. Initiates were helped by a snake and a dog, betrayed by a scorpion, and the triumphant conclusion of the rite was the plunging of a knife into a bull's neck. I thanked God for those Christians who had given their lives for us to have a much gentler, unbloody liturgy, though it seems so sad that man so quickly surrounded Christianity with viciousness, killing and persecution. I walked home past the Colosseum, along the Via dei Fori Imperiali as the traffic of Rome in a roar rushed here and there, with its different colours, homeward or pleasure bound. At the Anglican Centre in the evening, when thoroughly relaxed, it was such a delight to take off my shoes, slip on my slippers

and have the marvellous library in which to curl up with books and read about all that had happened in the day.

Wednesday 21 October

St John Lateran

The next day, after Eucharist using the simple Anglican Rite A, I set off by bus to explore St John Lateran, Rome's cathedral, *'Omnium urbis et orbis Ecclesiarum Mater et Caput'* ('Mother and head of the city of all people and of the world of churches'). The rather miserable baroque exterior decorated like a white birthday cake with little images on the top and fifteen statues, of Christ, John the Baptist, John the Evangelist and the twelve doctors of the Church, gives way to a rather shabby interior with the real feeling of

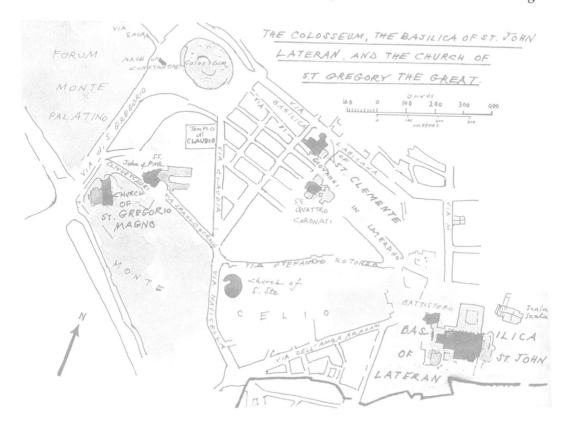

being a parish church, which I found friendly. Constantine gave it to Pope St Melchiades (AD 311–314) before he went to establish his new Rome at Constantinople, probably because he felt guilt-ridden at what he had done. When he came to the throne he had married two wives, the obscure Minervina who produced their heir to the throne Crispus, and Fausta who produced their sons Constantine II and Constans. There was much jealousy and intrigue and bitterness between the two families and Constantine had his son Crispus cold bloodedly murdered at Pola. To Fausta it seemed as if she had triumphed but the Empress mother, Helena, furious at the loss of her favourite grandson under suspicious circumstances, had Fausta suffocated, accidently on purpose, in the hot vapours of the Imperial baths. Constantine's great basilica had belonged to the rich patrician family of Plautius Lateranus who had been put to death by Nero following his involvement in a conspiracy. The property was brought as part of her marriage portion by Fausta to Constantine. He, following these dreadful events, gave it all away. The original five aisled church has had a chequered career, ruined by Vandals, restored by Pope Leo the Great (AD 440–461), upset by the earthquake of AD 896, enlarged and beau-

S. Giovanni in Laterano

tified greatly and reckoned at one time to be the wonder of the age, destroyed by fire in AD 1308 and again AD 1370. I warmed to it.

The sense of being in a living cathedral church was heightened by a notice of 'no admission' as three thousand chairs were being set out, together with television equipment, for the Diocesan Synod. Priests and religious were to be present, and to my delight Douglas Brown from the Anglican Centre was to be there as an observer. The confessionals were in use in Portugese, French and English, one priest looking rather bored and staring glumly at us all. I was not impressed by the ornate papal altar, on which only the Pope may say Mass. I loved the wooden table upon which St Peter, it is said, kept Eucharist, and on which Popes still celebrate facing East, but the canopy and Gothic Baldachino, etc. left me quite cold I'm afraid. I then walked round the south side of the basilica until I found the noble octagonal building of the Baptistry, built in the time of the Emperor Constantine. It was a little confusing at first because I thought the small green basalt bath was the place where the new Christians were bathed on Whitsun or Easter Day in the early church, but the real font was the whole great building itself, filled with water. What a remarkable sight it must have been, when a man of such spiritual stature as St Ambrose of Milan, for instance, after instructing his catachumens all through Lent, led them to such a font as this where, after they had declared their faith, they stripped naked and were plunged by the bishop, presbyters and presbytydies, 'In the name of the Father and of the Son and of the Holy Spirit' into the water. Rising out they would put on their white robes and walk to their new

S. Gregorio Magno

Christian way of life and receive their first communion. I missed hearing the singing doors! Apparently if you can get someone to move the famous bronze doors they make a strange tuneful sound.

Armed with my *Blue Guide* I was now ready to find the Church of St Gregorio Magno, one of my main aims while in Rome. It is situated on the Caelian Hill, the southernmost of the Seven Hills of Rome. I walked down the Via de Laterani until I came to the Via Ipponio and walked along one of the walls of Rome built by the Emperor Aurelian (Emperor AD 270–275). I continued on under the arch of the Porta Metronia and along the Via d Navicella beside pleasant lawns, following a signpost to St John and St Paul, and St Gregory the Great. I was beginning to need my lunch and siesta. At any rate I soon came to what I thought must be St Gregory the Great. A kindly English speaking priest of the Passionist order answered my knock on the door beside the church. I told him of my project and pilgrimage and he gave me a most encouraging blessing. But this was not St Gregory. That was next door! He pointed me on my way and told me to be sure to visit the fascinating Clivus Scauri and the Roman arches under which, in Roman times, the butcher, the baker and candlestick maker had their markets. Thinking again of lunch I made for home, determined to return in the afternoon.

Church of St Gregory the Great

After my siesta I followed the now familiar route along the Via dei Fori Imperiali to the Colosseum and the Arch of Constantine. I turned to the right along the Via di S Gregorio following no doubt the route taken so often by Gregory, Augustine and members of the community, until at last I could see the church standing on the hill. It is rather inaccessible and I had to walk past it towards the Piazza di Porta Capena and approach it from the other side. There it was, perhaps rather disappointing with its grimy steps, but it was to be for me as T.S. Eliot wrote:

> You are not here to verify, instruct yourself, or inform curiosity, or carry report, you are here to kneel. (Little Gidding in *Four Quartets*. Faber)

So up the steps I went. This of course is not the original mansion which had belonged to Gregory's father, Gordianus, a wealthy man of senatorial rank, and his mother Sylvia, which Gregory, when he had embraced the religious life, handed over to become a monastery naming it after St Andrew the apostle. Here in his

powerfully strict rule he at last became its abbot. How often he must have stood there and looked down on the Forum with all the associations such as I had imagined he would make, not least of the Emperor Constantine whom he had so much admired. The original church and the monastery was rebuilt by Pope Gregory II (AD 715–731) and transformed completely externally in 1629 by G.B. Soria for Cardinal Scipione Borghese, and internally in 1734 by F. Ferrari. In spite of the handsome baroque buildings which cluttered my mind, I tried to think of a simpler style that Gregory would perhaps have preferred. Through the gloom of the late afternoon I found framed pictures in modern script which I've re-drawn here, how on Saturday the 30 September 1989, Pope John Paul II attended vespers with Archbishop Robert Runcie, the full

This monastic church of St. Gregory has a particular significance for the English speaking world and for the ecumenical movement, since it was from here that St. Gregory the great towards the beginning of the seventh century sent two groups of monks to evangelize England; among the monks were St. Augustine, first Archbishop of Canterbury, St. Lawrence, St. Mellitus, St. Justus, and St. Onorius all succeeding archbishops of Canterbury, St. Paulinus, first archbishop of York.

The faithful who visit St. Gregory's Church are thus invited to remember in their prayers the reunion of all Christians.

text of their homilies to one another being so full of hope. The Pope wrote:

> In many parts of the developing world separated Christians are beginning to recognize and to act upon their baptismal unity, their one apostolic calling and their common obligation to proclaim the Gospel – in spite of an inheritance of Christian division not of their making.
>
> That disunity was made in Europe, the continent of Gregory and Augustine – disunity between East and West, Catholic and Protestant. It gravely impairs our ability to reclaim for Christ's Gospel a continent which is fast losing its Christian soul. We cannot rediscover European unity without reappropriating Europe's Christian roots.

and in their common declaration wrote:

> No pilgrim knows in advance all the steps along the path. Saint Augustine of Canterbury set out from Rome with his band of monks for what was then a distant corner of the world. Yet Pope Gregory was soon

'The stone on which Gregory slept.'

to write of the baptism of the English and of 'such great miracles ... that they seemed to imitate the powers of the apostles' (Letter of Gregory the Great to Eulogius of Alexandria). While we ourselves do not see a solution to this obstacle, we are confident that through our engagement with this matter our conversations will in fact help to deepen and enlarge our understanding. We have this confidence because Christ promised that the Holy Spirit, who is the Spirit of Truth, will remain with us forever (cf. John 14.16–17).

I unfortunately did not unearth the dedications of the quaint chapels on the left, described by Georgina Masson in her book. I saw the Salvati Chapel picture of the Virgin who is supposed to have spoken personally to Gregory, and the three chapels of St Andrew, St Sylvia and St Barbara. The first of these was Gregory's original oratory. There is also the table supposed to be that on which Gregory himself daily served meals to twelve poor men, and there are verses which record the legendary appearance of an angel who once made their number up to thirteen. Indeed, until 1870 the Popes on Maunday Thursday personally served thirteen pilgrims.

I then walked over to St Gregory's chapel in the far right hand corner of the church, looking at the fifteenth century

Questa Chiesa monastica di S. Gregorio ha un significato particolare per il mondo anglosassone, perchè fu da qui che S. Gregorio, verso l'inizio del settimo secolo, inviò due gruppi di monaci missionari per evangelizzare l'Inghilterra; fra questi monaci erano inclusi; S. Agostino, primo Arcivescovo di Canterbury, S. Laurentius, S. Mellitus S. Justus, e S. Onorius, tutti Arcivescovi successori di Canterbury, S. Paulinus, primo Arcivescovo di York, e S. Pietro, primo Abate dell'Abbazia di Canterbury.

I fedeli che visitano la Chiesa di San Gregorio sono quindi invitati a ricordare nelle loro preghiere la riunione di tutti i cristiani.

altar with its reliefs depicting scenes from his life, and I began to feel, like children playing hide and seek, that I was 'getting warm'. Right in the far corner I found Gregory's own chair, or episcopal throne, the stone upon which he slept in this nook which was his own cell. I loved to be deeply quiet there, and then, moved, took off my jacket and sat on Gregory's throne and made a meditation, for here indeed was a place of profound significance. I thought of Thanet, of Canterbury, of the long line of our Archbishops I had studied so often over the years, and of our kindly Church of England with its cathedrals and parish churches and all it stood for now. I thought of our gracious queen Elizabeth, a very English Constantine as Gregory would have said, of her empire, now shed of its former glory but still standing spiritually for something very stable in a very muddly world, and I gave thanks and prayed that this Pilgrimage may eventually mark a real turning point for the unity of all Christians, and men and women of good will who make up the English speaking world.

A Final Blessing

I then found my way to the Monastery of St Andrew, knocked boldly on the door and asked a young man who answered it if he could find for me an English speaking monk to whom I could talk. To my delight a leading director of the Benedictine order, a kindly and gracious Italian monk, Father Emanuele Bargellini, spoke English fluently. I told him, without stuttering too much I hope, of my longing for a blessing at this beginning of my pilgrimage to Canterbury. He was more than willing and left me to kneel by Gregory's chair in the gloom. Suddenly the lights came on over the

altar, a young man lit the candles, and after a while Father Emanuele came with his white Benedictine habit on and stood by me and we spoke comfortably of what I was planning to do. He then went to the altar, took out the great Mass Book, read out the gospel about Jesus sending out his disciples on their journey, we prayed and then to my joy he sprinkled me with Holy Water and gave me a final blessing. It was all so encouraging and I hope all pilgrims setting off from here to Canterbury will feel so deeply spiritual, happy and at peace with the world. I do thank him for his gestures. I walked home quietly and thoughtfully past the Colosseum, along the wide empty street of the Via dei Fori Imperiali in the gloaming while the traffic roared along the roads, the motor cycles screamed and the trams clattered by and all the bright colours of white, gold and red came on. Rome was going home for the evening.

Gregory's Chair in the monastery of St Andrew

Basilica of St Maria Maggiore

Thursday 22 October

Santa Maria Maggiore

This day I planned to go to the great patriarchal church of Santa Maria Maggiore, built on the top of the Esquiline Hill. I was longing to see it because there Gregory, as the sneezing fit plague raged in Rome in AD 590, had been captured and consecrated as Pope against his will, addressed the people and told them that their only hope for Rome was to give up their wickedness and like Jonah who had done penance to Ninevah, they must travel in penance. Straight to the point, on the next Wednesday Gregory said all were to go in procession, chanting litanies and pleading to God for forgiveness. He arranged that from their various stations all were to meet together at St Maria Maggiore, the basilica of the Blessed Virgin Mary, Mother of our Lord Jesus Christ; the priests from St Cosmas Damian (in the Forum), the abbots and monks from SS Protasius and Gervasius, the Abbesses from Marcellinus, the children from John and Paul, (under his own eye as it were, near his St Gregorio Magno), the laymen from St Stephen, the widows from St Euphemia, and the married women from St Clement. It must have been a most impressive sight. Eighty people fell down dead as the procession passed chanting its litanies with their curt 'Good Lord, deliver us' or 'Kyrie Eleison'. However, it worked, and the plague ceased. It was the beginning of a completely new era, that time which has come to be known as the Middle Ages with all its achievements and tragedies. Even today on our Rogation walks to bless church, crops and houses on the fifth Sunday after Easter we say as responses to prayers 'Good Lord, deliver us' and it leaves a powerful impression.

I wonder if all those embarking on the pilgrimage to Canterbury could meet in groups as they did then, to continue on their way together in quiet reverence. Augustine and his companions as they neared Canterbury sang this litany:

We beseech thee O Lord, in all thy mercy, that
thy anger and wrath be turned away from this city,
and from thy holy house, because we have sinned. Hallelujah. (Bede, Book I.25)

I entered the great basilica of Santa Maria Maggiore which is so graceful and of magnificent size, quite dwarfing the people inside it. It was built by Pope Sixtus III in AD 432–440 after his visionary prayers, firstly because many Roman matrons continued to find their way here to offer prayers to the mother goddess Juno Lucina, and secondly because of a rather scandalous series of interruptions and argument which led to the third General Council of Ephesus (428–431). The orthodox clergy and people generally, however, accepted the faith of Nicaea, and when thinking of Jesus as being born as the 'Eternal-word-of-God-made-flesh', spoke of Mary as the 'Mother of God', but Nestorius, who was

said to be a fine preacher, would not admit that a child of two or three months could be 'God'. It was clear that many people must have felt deeply confused, but it was one of those occasions where the finer points of theological debate were overwhelmed by the deep commonsense of ordinary people. In the end, amongst much rejoicing, the Orthodox and Catholic clergy agreed that Jesus, the very flesh and blood child of the Virgin Mary, was the Eternal Word written of by St John. The Emperor Theodosius II deposed Nestorius and since then all the branches of the Church at large have upheld the Council's conclusions.

When Pope Sixtus III received the news of the outcome of the Council he was so delighted that he began to build the great basilica which was then dedicated to the Blessed Virgin Mary, and it is certainly full of feminine grace. There is a charming legend that Pope Liberius (AD 352–366) was standing on the site on 5 August. He received a vision from the Virgin Mary that he should build a basilica there, and that morning snow fell and marked out the site. Every year on the date of the snowfall white petals are dropped into the church at the Mass. I felt the whole place looked jolly, and as I went in, there is only one word for my feelings – joy. There is the holy crib, the presepio, known to have been in existence since AD 642. It is a good experience merely to stand and look at it and accept it all quite simply as a child, and to imagine the chant. It is quite breathtaking and it is well worth while to take with you Georgina Masson's *Companion Guide to Rome* (pp. 284-287), though I was not ready to take in all the skill of the architecture or even of the acheiropoieton picture of the Madonna. On entering I could not believe that this great basilica had largely remained the same from its beginning, with its great columns, although clearly its roof had been repaired and improved. It was exciting to be actually walking on the mosaics on the floor decorated by Sixtus III that Gregory and Augustine must often have walked on. There was such a galaxy there both to see and to imagine. I could picture that day, 25 April AD 590 when the great procession crossed over the Tiber on its way here, and saw the sight of the Archangel Michael with his sword to stay the plague of Rome, and how everyone was overwhelmed with joy.

St Pudenziana

After my siesta I really had a most exciting afternoon. I had been reading H.V. Morton's book *A Traveller in Rome* (p. 210) and was determined to find the church of St Pudenziana, and then if I could, to look for what nobody seems to know much about, S. Martino ai Monti. For if I was to start from S. Martino ai Monti, it seemed good to end my pilgrimage at St Martin on the hill outside the city wall of Canterbury. I took the no. 70 bus and got out at the Piazza del Esquilino outside Santa Maria Maggiore. I was in for two surprises. I walked across the Piazza del Esquilino, over the Via Cavour to the Via Urbana and there, most strangely, was the house church of St Pudenziana as H.V. Morton described, with its battered orange plaster and twenty two steps down from the street to enter. This church has long been believed to be the oldest place of Christian worship in Rome. How refreshing it was to escape from so much of the baroque with which I had been surrounded with all its rather overdone glossiness, and to find some-

St Pudenziana

thing so simple and original, just as the early Christians would have known it. According to legend, and here I was quick to accept it as fact, hook, line and sinker, that the house was one of those great senatorial mansions belonging to the senator Pudens and his daughters Prassede and Pudenziana whom St Peter converted and with whom he lived for seven years. Research seems to have made it clear that at the base of the church in the second century a bathing place was discovered, a hundred years after Peter's death. Recently archaeologists maintain that the whole building had been originally some baths, though I, my mind full of the traditional explanation like to think of it as a large font. Certainly dedicatory inscriptions confirm it as a church of the time of St Siricius (Pope AD 384–399). The wonder of the church is the fifth century mosaic. However, I find it easy to think of the house church St Paul mentioned – in his second epistle to Timothy:

> Eubulus greeteth thee, and Pudens, and Linus, and Claudia and all the brethren. (2 Tim 4.21)

There was one relic found there, an ancient chair said to be the senatorial chair of Pudens and used by St Peter as his episcopal throne. This is now one of the locked away treasures of St Peter's. The other relic, the wooden table on which it was believed St Peter celebrated the Eucharist, has been enclosed for centuries within the High Altar of St John Lateran. I could easily think of St Peter with Pudens and his senatorial family worshipping together, as I believe that ecumenical house churches are the way forward for our churches to grow together today.

While I was there, there was a group of some thirty or forty people with their priest in the nave, celebrating the Eucharist and singing in harmony quite perfectly in some language I could not understand. I could not but hope that this church might be a venue where all Christians could meet for worship, and though divided, be allowed to keep eucharist together like that group I watched. I hoped, too, that other ancient places of worship such as our own St Martin's in Canterbury could be used for ecumenical Eucharistic worship.

S. Martino ai Monti

Out in the open again I was in for quite a walk, some 360 metres as the crow flies, for in spite of the *Blue Guide* I lost my way through fascinating by-streets, many of them rather dilapidated, past a man sitting making a black suit with a needle and thread, past men sawing wood and making furniture, and past garages. Nobody seemed to know of S. Martino ai Monti, or perhaps I was not clear in my questioning. Suddenly a strident bell began to ring at 5.20pm, bong, bong, bong! I found the church, and the bell had its own special red brick tower. Inside the church I saw a group of elderly people chatting together as they walked, making for vespers, just as at St Martin's at Canterbury, and I realised how powerful these two or threes of elderly Christians are. I joined them, the bell stopped, and a woman's voice began singing Vespers in Italian (was it on cassette,) and the old ladies mumbled the answers. As I looked around the basilica of S. Martino ai Monti I must say I was rather deflated by the splendid gilded Renaissance ceiling, for the whole baroque building was rebuilt around AD 1650 on the site of the original Titulus Equitii, or house church, the first church on the site being built by St Sylvester (Pope AD 314–335) and restored and enlarged by Pope Symmachus (AD 498–514). Strangely enough the original building, rather like St Pudenziana had close connections with baths, as round the back of the church are the great blocks of rock which probably formed part of the Baths of Trajan.

What did fascinate me, however, was that the original Roman house was made into a church under the direction of Pope Sylvester I, and taken under the patronage of Constantine. Some time after Constantine's tragic family killings (see Wednesday 21 October – St John Lateran) he was struck down with leprosy and no art could cure him. In the end he called for Pope Sylvester who was hiding at Mount Soracte. The old pope gave him consolation and absolution, and was ever afterwards associated with Constantine. As a result it was on this site, in the presence of Constantine himself, that the decisions of the Council of Nicaea were proclaimed to the Roman Empire, and all the heretical-books of Arius, Sabellius and Victorinus publicly burnt. On this venerable site Pope Symmachus caused the basilica to be rebuilt and for some reason dedicated it to St Martin of Tours.

I could not find out why, but it may have been because of the powerful development of respect for Martin as the champion of the Nicene faith, for his healing powers and for his reputation as always being on the side of the underdog. The church has been changed five times, and because of the vespers I could not go probing around under the high altar and look for the crypt which contains, it is said, the relics of many martyrs. I walked home in the evening along by the Colosseum and the Via dei Fori Imperiali, fascinated by it all, and knowing there was so much to see that I would never have time to be able to understand the glory and tragedy that was Rome.

Basilica of S. Martino ai Monti

Friday 23 October

After Matins and breakfast I was writing up my diary, happily thinking of my plans and of how I intended to spend a day at the Vatican and St Peter's. I was due to leave on the Sunday to start the return to Canterbury. For that journey I was to have a good companion with a car. I had arranged with Father Douglas to have a young Italian student to accompany me who was making his first visit to London. News came that day that he could not come and I must confess that because of my deafness I was rather alarmed. However, what with the prayers of those in England to comfort me, and Father Douglas' assurance that he would look after me wherever I was, I went on with my plans. I planned to go on the Saturday to visit the Catacombs. Although being on my own had been such a marvellous experience, I realise now that things began to go wrong. I successfully found a travel agent who gave me my ticket to get to Nice on Sunday, ready for me to go on to Cannes and Lérins and the community of St Honorat.

I now asked a man how to get to St Peter's and he said I was to get on the famous 65 bus. I was agog and stood on it in the swaying crowd as we banged over the cobbles. Staring out of the window I found no River Tiber, no Castello Sant' Angelo, but we rattled on interminably until suddenly there again were those two white marble horses of the Vittorio Emmanuele II monument. I had clearly gone in the wrong direction. It started to pour with rain so after luncheon and a good siesta I stayed indoors and caught up with my writing.

I never did see any of the catacombs

The Catacombs

which was a great disappointment, and I had to content myself by reading about them in, among other books, the *Encyclopaedia Britannica* (eleventh edition) when I got home. I also dug out again that book which had made such a profound impression on me when I was young, called *Marius the Epicurean*, by Walter Pater (first published in 1885 and now in Penguin Classics 1985). Pater was educated, like me, at the King's School in Canterbury, and though the book is Victorian and rather long winded, the description of the Eucharist in the catacombs (p. 246 ff) is charming and deeply moving.

The name catacomb originally bore no connection with burial, but was simply the name of a certain part of the ground in a hollow in Rome, lying close to the Appian Way, and derived from the Greek $K\alpha\tau\alpha$ – down, $K\nu\mu\beta\eta$ – hollow vessel. At the time of the great persecutions thousands of Christian martyrs, many of their names remembered, lived in deep vaults, creating in the end a sort of vast under-croft beneath Rome. St Jerome (AD 331–420) who translated the Vulgate, visited them as a youth and wrote:

> When I was a boy receiving my education in Rome, I and my school fellows used, on Sundays, to make the circuit of the sepulchres of the apostles and martyrs. Many a time did we go down into the catacombs. These are excavated deep in the earth, and contain, on either hand as you enter, the bodies of the dead buried in the wall. It is all so dark there that the language of the prophet seems to be fulfilled . . . 'Let them go down quick into hell' (Psalm 55.15). Only occasionally is light let in to mitigate the horror of the gloom, and then not so much through a hole. You take each step with caution . . .

Today it is the same, as you will see as you meet at the Catacombs of St Callisto, or beneath the basilica of St Sebastiano, or the vast Catacombs of St Calixtus. H.V. Morton describes how, as you walk around in the group of pilgrims carrying your candle, and you will see the remarkable paintings and evidences of the Eucharistic ceremonies performed for instance, on the table tombs.

I was desperately sad not to be able to find the Appian Way and a catacomb, in order to feel in close touch with the inspiration of those Christians who had traded in their lives and pain for Jesus and for eternal life.

Saturday 24 October

On this my last day in Rome I was again determined to go over the Tiber, to see at any rate, the Castello Sant' Angelo and to find St Peter's itself. This time I did get it right, with the number 65 bus going the right way! Soon it started to pour with rain, but through the clouds I could see a scrap of blue in the wan sky. There was the Tiber. We climbed down out of the bus and were there, standing in the great Piazzo, bemused by Bernini's (AD 1656–67) masterpiece and far in the distance was the world's largest basilica, with the people all walking about, looking from

A chamber in the Roman catacombs

this distance like ants. There are 284 columns and 88 pilasters all around it and on the Ionic entablature 96 massive statues of saints and martyrs. In the middle is the obelisk of the Vatican, and on either side, magnificent fountains. I saw, too, how most of the square was filled with seats ready, I supposed, for the people who would be waiting for the pope to give his blessings. For some reason, I don't think it was only the rain, I became more and more disgruntled at the grandeur of it all when I remembered those mansions or house churches or catacombs. I remembered again Arthur Hugh Clough's poem:

> Rome disappoints me much, — St Peter's perhaps in especial ... This, however, perhaps is the weather, which is truly horrid!

To begin with the very size of it shows what an incredible achievement it is. You need to realise that it was all begun by the Emperor Constantine. It seems that there had been an oratory built there in AD 90, over the tomb of St Peter, close to Nero's circus. The Emperor Constantine asked Pope Sylvester I to build a basilica 120 metres long and 65 metres wide there, and it was consecrated on 18 November AD 326. In the fifteenth century it began to show signs of collapse, and from then on some of the most prestigious architects and artists in the world were asked to work on it.

The moment you go in the first thing to do is to get one of the excellent leaflets called 'Vatican City', which is completely free. It is possible to go round easily, not only the basilica but the Apostolic Palace and the museums. For pilgrims bound for Canterbury, at any rate for me, the highlight was to find St Gregory's altar where I prayed. I looked at the beautiful thirteenth century statue of St Peter by Arnolfo di Cambio, and tried to come to terms with Michaelangelo's Pieta. I sat a long time waiting while a group of elderly people in white and black costumes, the

'View of S. Pietro Basilica (centre dome), seen in the rain as I crossed the Tiber in a buse.'

men with their smart bow ties, prepared to sing, and a crowd gathered, but nothing happened. I wondered whether all this vast expense and play acting was really what Christ wants of us all, but I was certain it would have cheered the Emperor Constantine and, I suppose by the same token, St Gregory. I went out into the pouring rain under a lowering sky, there were suddenly claps of thunder which made everyone run for protection, and it somehow seemed fitting.

Back on the bus I began to think about the Castello Sant' Angelo. I would not have time to go over it all, but as the bus ground over the Tiber I wiped away the condensation from the window and could see it. I managed to snatch a quick photograph of it with the pale blue sky against the dark clouds, and a glimpse of the angel with its sheathed sword right on the top. As we drove in the bus across the Tiber I remembered again how St Gregory of Tours' deacon Agiulf, who was present at the procession, said that while the people were making their supplication to the Lord, eighty individuals fell dead to the ground. The Pope never once stopped preaching to the people, nor did the people pause in their prayers. In the meantime, tradition has it, on 25 April AD 590 as the procession reached the bridge over the Tiber, the Archangel Michael appeared on the dome of Hadrian's mausoleum with a flaming sword in his hand. He sheathed his sword and so put an end to the plague.

When I set out to visit Rome and to find out all the Gregory sites, it seemed that time and time again I saw how Gregory had been shadowing Britain and now, as I was leaving, I realised this perhaps more strongly than before. For that huge circular tower right on the bank of the Tiber was begun by one of the most capable Emperors that ever occupied the throne. This was 'our' Hadrian, who on one of his journeys through the Empire came to Britain and in the spring of AD 122 personally supervised the building of 'Hadrian's Wall', the rampart which stretches from the Tyne to the Solway. After all his great military journeyings, and he certainly was a remarkable man, he wrote prose and verse and composed an autobiography. As he was waiting to die he wrote his charming:

> *Animula vagula, blandula*
> *Hospes comesque corporis,*
> *Quae nunc abidas in loca*
> *Pallidula, rigida, nudala,*
> *Nec, at soles, dabis jocos?*

which so many people have tried to translate, and which I could not forbear trying also:

> My old body's friend
> Now you are off to some unknown place,
> Leaving me pale and rigid and stripped,
> No more jokes now as we used to have.

His ashes and those of his wife Sabina were laid at the Castello Sant' Angelo and as the years made the mausoleum more magnificent, the ashes of Antoninus, Marcus Aurelius and Septimius Severus, who knew his Britain so well, went there too. It seemed to me as if in this area over the River Tiber, Gregory's own dreams and visions of Britain and England were all bound up together in the visions of Hadrian, Antoninus and Severus in some way.

The Castello Sant' Angelo now contains the Museo Nazionale de Castello Sant' Angelo, consisting of three floors, the third being the Papal Apartments, with an unrivalled view of the whole of Rome from the top. The military and artistic museum seems to me to need a whole day or more to study, and much walking! Among other things the place was used by Theodoric, king of the Ostrogoths (AD 454–526) as a prison, and as the years went by it became more and more a place where torturing, imprisonment, starving to death and every indescribable pain were inflicted, according to lurid contemporary accounts.

After my final siesta in Rome I made my preparations to continue my pilgrimage to Canterbury. I was only too conscious of my shortcomings as a pilgrim since I was old, on my own, doing it all on the cheap, and having to travel by bus or by train. The trains in France, though good timekeepers and comfortable, are extremely fast and do not want to dawdle. I realise now more and more that my description of the pilgrimage is but that of a path-finder, for those others coming after me to improve on as they savour the enjoyments of the route. So here are a few ideas to help other pilgrims. First, if the pilgrim is to travel alone by land, sea and air, it is necessary to have one of those folding nylon shopping trolleys with wheels. Secondly, know a smattering of French and Italian. For me a little more of both would have helped. How wonderful it would have been to cycle the pilgrimage – but oh! to be young would have been very heaven. Travel more sedately by car with a caravan or stay in pensions along the way, found by using one of Fodor's fine travel guides *Affordable France* or *Affordable Italy*.

For me it will be wonderful enough to think of those many millions that I hope will make this pilgrimage in the centenary year of 1997, setting off from all over the world, say by coach in groups of different denominations, growing together spiritually into a new kind of Christian unity as they travel. A sensitive courier could make sure there is time for silence and meditation and encourage singing on the journey, something that Gregory loved. I have made clear maps to show how the pilgrimage might develop, though obviously there will be endless pleasant debate about it all by the pundits. To go direct to France by sea from Rome at Ostia is impossible. The road is the only alternative to travelling by air. This Roman road, whose origin is unknown, the Via Aurelia, follows the coast via Genoa, Nice, Cannes, Aix-en-Provence to Arles. I would have loved to have travelled by rail or road to Piombino and then by ferry, seeing Elba and thinking of Napoleon; spending a night on Corsica at Bastia with its many churches dedicated to Columban and then sailing across the Mediterranean to Nice, enjoying the coastline. As it was, after Eucharist and breakfast on that last morning Father Douglas and Serge, a young student, found me a taxi to the airport. I said 'arrivederci' to Rome and was soon airborne bound for Nice.

CHAPTER SIX

The Pilgrimage Route to England

FLYING for me has always been a delight and now, perhaps, more than ever as I was on my way home. No one will ever really know how Augustine and his companions travelled from Rome to their next destination at the island of Lérins off Cannes, but I am sure before they set off that the whole group was given by Gregory most solemn missionary benedictions. I had received my benedictions both at their monastery on the Caelian Hill in St Andrew's church, and from St Peter's Basilica.

I can imagine that after their blessings they packed all their baggage into carts and trundled along the Via Aurelia, with a posse of well-wishers accompanying them for part of the way, until they were thoroughly alarmed by the Lombards who halted them at Piombino. Anyway, as Bede recounts, 'on their journey they were seized with a sudden fear, and began to think of returning home rather than proceed to a barbarous, fierce and unbelieving nation whose very language was strange to them. This they unanimously agreed was the safest course. They sent back Augustine with a plea to Pope Gregory . . . that they should not be compelled to undertake so dangerous toilsome and uncertain a journey'. This story has already been told in chapter one. Poor Augustine struggled back to his companions now appointed by Gregory as their abbot, which meant that they were now under obligations and vows of total obedience in all things! There was to be no nonsense and they must get on quickly to the island of Lérins where Gregory had prepared enter-

tainment and encouragement for the mission, by Abbot Stephen.

As the aircraft rose thrillingly into the sky it was lovely to look down on the Mediterranean Sea for the first time, at the ever changing colours of cobalt, ultramarine and cerulean blues, and in the distance the coastline of Italy and the island of Elba, just off the coast from Piombino. I could see the island of Corsica and the town of Bastia all standing out clearly. I could not help thinking of Augustine and his companions bewildered by the strangeness and dangers ahead, and how they must have longed to be back in Rome, while here was I, flying over this glorious and spiritually uplifting scene on my way home.

The neat Alitalia stewards and stewardesses provided a charming luncheon, and before very long we were gliding down towards Nice, and I was in France. Coming out of the airport there was a waiting bus whose sign showed Cannes as its destination. I was soon in the bus and on my way to Cannes, ready for the island of Lérins, where I had long before

The route from Rome to Bastia

made arrangements to stay at the Abbaye de Lérins Hotellerie, on the island of Saint Honorat (F-06406–Cannes). In France I could at least hold some kind of conversation; the friendly bus driver, when I showed him the tarifs I had obtained from the Tourist Office (Palais des Festivals, La Croisette, Tel: 93–39–24–53), assured me to my delight that there would be a boat ready to take me to the island. Soon I was on the quay and there was the boat. It was by now a beautifully sunny evening, but there was a full gale blowing. I went to the office to pay for the ticket, but to my chagrin, probably because of the high wind, the woman most volubly said there was no sailing today. *'Mais je desire aller'*, I said, *'rester avec les moins a St Honorat!'*. The answer was decisively *'NON, non, non!'*, so the only thing to do was to get out my *Affordable France* to find some suggestions about lodging, though I learned one should always check the cost! After the comparative cheapness of Italy and its thousands of paper lire I found that after using my VISA card all the way, my VISA statement from the bank when I got home made me jump! France is more expensive than Italy.

I found some excellent lodgings and was treated, travel worn as I must have looked, like a lord. I went for a walk along the Boulevard de la Croisette, and in spite of the gale was fascinated by the superb beautiful young ladies, who all seemed blonde Venuses, and the Adonis like young men. I found the Gare Maritime and the marinas with all the yachts lying in rows cheek by jowl, some with red carpets inviting the wealthy to come in and have a drink. After a good dinner with the maitre d'hotel to wait on my every wish, I went to a most luxurious bed to read. What I should have done again was to read the account that Gregory received from Stephen the Abbot of Lérins. It was clear that Gregory had sent presents or money to defray the expenses of such a large group of monks descending on the already overcrowded small island.

> From Gregory to Stephen, Abbot of Lérins.
> We were rejoiced by the account which Augustine, the servant of God, the bearer of these presents, gave us, when he related that you kind sir, are, as you should be, on the watch, affirming also that the presbyters and deacons and the whole congregation are living in unanimity. (Mason)

After warning them about the devil, he ends with this enigmatic note:

> The spoons and plates which you despatched have come safely to hand, and we thank your charity, because you have shown how you love the poor, by sending for their use the articles which they require. (Mason)

I longed to go over the next day by boat to St Honorat and keep my planned two days retreat there, but it was not to be. The wind howled and the lady in the ticket office was so adamant: 'No St Honorat', but I could go to the nearer island of of Lérins St Marguerite. I was frustrated indeed, but got on the boat with some children and their parents and we set off for St Marguerite, banging over the waves. I felt exhilarated by the journey in the hot sun with the blue, white and red tricolour flag streaming out behind us. St Marguerite is a large rather barren sandy island, old fashioned and untidy with shabby restaurants, and the place where the mysterious 'man-in-the-iron-mask' was imprisoned. In among the eucalyptus and pine trees it struck me as a very sad place. Later as I sat on the train on the way to Marseille I gazed out to sea and saw the other little island clearly, St Honorat, where I had longed to stay. But perhaps one day I may go there, who knows? The brothers sent me a copy of the delightful brief history excellently illustrated that would make anyone who reads it long to go there, and I have here brought together a description of how it came to be founded.

To be publicly martyred was a kind of joy to many of the early Christians because, after the disgrace and pain there was the promise of everlasting joy with Christ. St Stephen, the first martyr, even while being stoned saw the glory of God and Jesus standing at His right hand. Now, however, after the Emperor Constantine had ceased the persecutions of the Christians in AD 315, there was no chance of testifying in this way, of proving their belief in everlasting life, so there began a great exodus of zealous Christians into the deserts of Egypt and Palestine, to live their whole lives in absolute poverty as celibates. In short, they became known as Monks, or loners for Christ. Among them the most famous was St Anthony of Egypt who lived alone in a ruined castle and fought there with the devils which beset his mind. It was not long before thousands followed his example, but some finding the loneliness was driving them mad, made for themselves congregations or monasteries to live as Christ had taught, following a rule of absolute poverty and giving away anything over and above their most basic

St Honorat, Lérins

requirements. Soon, all over southern Gaul the simple monastic communities sprang up, like that of St Martin or John Cassian, whose group at Marseilles (founded c. AD 415) was said to have five thousand brothers and whose marvellous constitutions and collations fascinated the then whole world, and ours too where they are known about.

St Honorat was a Gaul, who after a visit from Marseilles to the East, returned to Provence and in AD 410 moved with a friend to live on the little island of Lérins. Very quickly the monastic life developed until there were hundreds of followers, and St Honorat caused them to be made into a congregation with chosen presbyters to help them. Some lived in groups, while the more advanced hermits had small chapels or cells to live in. Honorat eventually was persuaded to leave Lérins and become bishop of Arles. It seems to me that, through the loneliness and spirituality of monasticism it often quickly develops a mission to convert the heathen. Many famous monks came to live in Lérins, like St Vincent of Lérins (died 450) whose threefold test of Christian orthodoxy is still believed by the Church universal:

> ... what is still believed everywhere, what is believed by always and what is believed by everyone.

St Hilary took over as bishop of Arles when Honorat died. St Benedict Biscop, an English monk, was trained here at Lérins. In AD 681 he established the monastery at Jarrow where later the Venerable Bede lived, and it was from Bede that our account in his *History of the English People* was taken. There is a strong tradition that St Patrick spent time at St Martins at Tours and Marmoutier

A cell on Lérins

before travelling on to Lérins to train for his mission to Ireland. Over time, Lérins St Honorat and the island gradually fell into sad disorder and in the eighth century was destroyed by raiding Saracens. After the French Revolution it was put up for sale by auction. In 1859 it was sold to the bishop of Frejus and in 1869 the Cistercian order of monks took it over again and is still a thriving community. Strict obedience is observed, and there is solitary and common prayer centred on the Eucharist in the lovely abbey church. Manual work is done each day in silence, and visitors are welcome to wander around the island and buy the handicrafts or liqueurs for sale there. For visitors there is not only the Grand Masse every Sunday at 10.45am, but a monastic museum, and retreats are organised all through the year. Often in the evenings a Son-et-Lumière is put on. The telephone of the Abbey is 93 48 68 68.

I was so frustrated at not having those two retreat days I had planned at Lérins St Honorat, where the guestmaster had been so ready to make me welcome at the

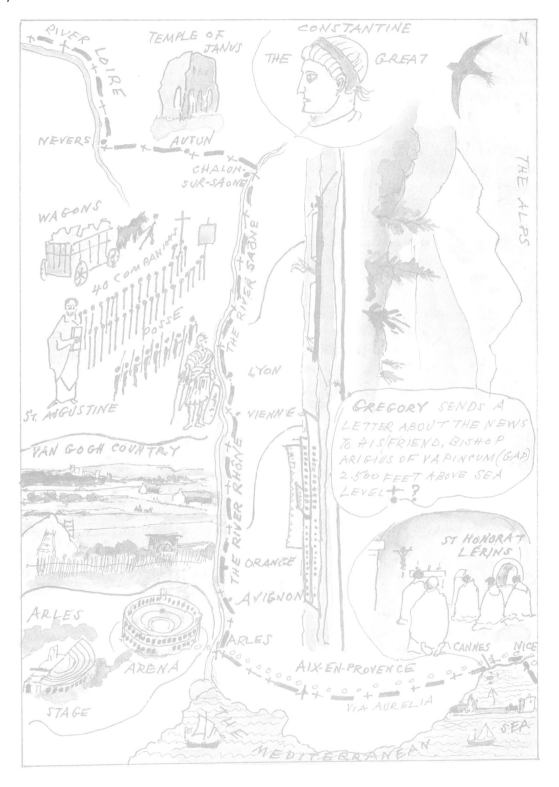

The route from Lérins to Nevers

hotellerie. I had been looking forward to reading their books, idling about and just being alone with such companions in the quiet, with no fuss. It would have been so good to relax and sleep, walk and read, after the Eucharist. But there we are. It did not happen. Looking ahead to the next leg of the journey I had two possibilities before me. The first was to travel along the Via Aurelia to Aix-en-Provence, for certainly Gregory had suggested to Augustine and his group that he should do that, and stay there. My other possibility was to travel by train along the coast to Marseilles and so directly to Arles. In the end I did the latter as it seemed the simplest, and Arles was beckoning me.

Arles is such a powerful Christian place. Here the Emperor Constantine at one time had his principal residence and he made it the ecclesiastical primatial province for the whole of Gaul. The early synods, such as that of AD 314, were held there. The S.N.C.F. train took me to Marseilles where I changed for Arles. The trouble with these trains, as far as I am concerned, is that they go so fast through the beautiful countryside, I could not take it all in and therefore did not enjoy it as much as I might. There were along the coast inlets with cliffs, boats moored, sand and always the open sea, the Mediterranean, and it was just as beautiful as the holiday brochures say. Marseilles is said to be the maritime melting pot of the world, where the Rhône flows into the sea. It was founded as a port by the Greeks around 600 BC. I did not stop there longer than I need because I felt it would be raucous and with its old docks and fishing boats, smelly, though I gather it has a fine Musée de l'Histoire de Marseilles exhibiting a large Roman boat.

Those pilgrims who choose to go by road along the Via Aurelia from Cannes to Aix-en-Provence travel as Augustine did. Gregory had sent letters of encouragement and cash ahead of the missionaries to the local bishops Protasius of Aix and Vergilius of Arles to help pay for the support and maintenance of such a large group when they descended on them. Gregory in one of his letters is quick to praise Protasius:

> Your great love for the blessed Peter, the chief of the Apostles . . . We have learned by what Augustine, the servant of God, the bringer of these presents, tells us. Bid Vergilius, our brother and fellow bishop, to be sure to remit to us the payments which his predecessor for many years got in from our poor estate and kept by him, because they are the property of the poor . . . We commend to your Holiness our common son, the presbyter Candidus, to whom we have entrusted the estate. (Mason)

Gregory's agent and presbyter at Marseilles, Candidus, had certainly been full of activity for the mission in the whole of Gaul. He had taken the opportunity to follow up and collect any papal revenues or defaultings that had been going on.

Augustine and his group would have come to Aix-en-Provence, the gateway to the whole area of the Rhône, Saône and Loire valleys which as everyone knows can be quite idyllic. Aix-en-Provence is an important educational centre, the seat of the faculties of law and letters of the University. It was the first Roman settlement in Gaul and was founded by Caius Sextius soon after a battle with the local tribe in 121 BC and was named Aquae Sextiae. One of its great claims to fame is the thermal springs which still bring people from far and wide. The bathing establishment was built in 1705 near the site of the ancient baths of Sextius of which vestiges still exist. The Cathédrale St Sauveur is a 'mishmash of styles and lacks harmony', but on the right is the early Christian baptistry (6th century and renovated in 1577) and behind the altar is the chapelle de St Mitre (5th century). Any pilgrim following in the footsteps of St Augustine who passes through this place can keep Eucharist there and pray where he prayed. The art enthusiast might wish to venture to the north of the old town to visit the studio of Paul Cézanne, complete with his pipe, and an audio-visual display.

At Marseilles I changed onto a local train for Arles. After a while of slipping through the great concrete city of Marseilles there was the Rhône itself, this marvellous mighty waterway along which Augustine and his group were almost certainly towed. They would have gone to Chalon, thence by road to Autun for the hundred and sixty kilometres or so to Nevers. They would then have floated down by barge to Tours. In amongst the trees and fields I saw a glimpse of a man on a tractor, digging potatoes and the dark cypresses everywhere made me feel I was already in Van Gogh country. We soon arrived in Arles.

Armed with my *Affordable France* I quickly found the lodging provided by St Trophime which at one time had been part of a cloister, next door to the church (16 Rue Calade, 13200, tel. 90 96 28 05, closed mid November to mid December and most of January). It was here that Vergilius, the bishop of Arles received a strong letter from Gregory:

> . . . exert yourself spontaneously in causes pleasing to God . . . Therefore we inform your holiness that we have by the Lord's providence sent to those parts, for the sake of souls, Augustine, a servant of God, whose zeal and earnestness is well known to us, along with other servants of God, as he will be able to inform you face to face. In this matter you must help him with prayer with us, brother, pray consider our recommendation of the presbyter Candidus, our common son, and the poor estate belonging to our church, that by your holiness's help the poor may derive some profit and maintenance from it. Your predecessor held that estate for many years . . .

Gregory then goes on:

> It is a very detestable thing that what has been preserved by the King's of the Nations should be said to have been diverted by the bishops. (Mason)

In short Gregory seems to have been very cross indeed. At the same time he wrote to Arigius the Patrician of Gaul whose government centre was probably here, asking for 'encouragement' for the group as they went through Gaul, presumably in the form of barges, baggage waggons and an armed escort.

The St Trophime lodgings were excellent and I treated myself to some really wonderful cooking. Afterwards I wandered about the place which seemed so intriguing, bought two excellent well illustrated small guide books that give all the information a pilgrim could need, and also a lovely, brightly coloured little book on 'Van Gogh in the land of Arles'. As I lay in bed I enjoyed reading the books. Arles is wonderful. I read that the Phoenicians and the Greeks in turn settled here and, joined by Gaulish tribes eventually gave rise to a new civilisation. In 49 BC Julius Caesar subdued the whole area. Under the emperors Augustus and Constantine the city became the second capital of the Roman world, with seven

The Amphitheatre, Arles

routes meeting there, the Via Aurelia from Rome and the Via Agrippa following up north along the Rhône. Gradually I went off to sleep soundly!

The next day I soon realised just how Roman Arles is. It was not difficult to visualise it in its heyday when Augustine and his companions stayed there. The quite beautiful, fairly cheap, glossy guides show the Amphitheatre, like a mini Colosseum, where the gladiators fought and, no doubt, the Christians lived in mortal dread of persecution. Just for good measure I sat on one of the seats and looked down on the sand covered arena where even today bull fights are held. Then there was the quite exquisite Roman theatre which could accommodate twelve thousand spectators with such perfect acoustics that all could hear the play. I spent a long time in the museum of pagan art where I saw the bust of Augustus and the mosaics from Roman houses. I then went to the most extraordinary museum of Christian art, one of the most famous in the early Christian world. How

Augustine and his companions must have loved such as the 'Constantine' sarcophagus from the crypt of St Honorat (AD 429), on which all the apostles are represented, with two soldiers separating them. The many tombs all around make one understand how enthusiastic the Christians were now that they were freed from persecution by Constantine.

I had not time to find the Champs Elysée or Alyscamps, the ancient Christian cemetery. In the evening I did go to the Eucharist at the great church of St Trophime (1152–1180) and receive a blessing from the priest for my pilgrimage. I felt much at home. Since Vatican II our Eucharists have grown together. The priest seemed to be wondering why I was only asking for a blessing rather than partaking of the Eucharistic bread and wine. My halting French did not help my attempts at explanation. I loved the bowl of fragrant incense which was brought in, which made me imagine I might have been in Bemerton church with George Herbert!

Arles café evening

I sat in the restaurant and had a lovely supper – Tagialle Samorn – tapioca and salmon with an excellent sauce, fruit and a glass of wine. I came to the conclusion that Augustine's pilgrimage from Rome to Canterbury might likewise have had its compensations. Before going to bed I again read some of the lovely book I had bought on Van Gogh in the land of Arles and thought how my restaurant supper scene was not unlike his own picture 'Cafe evening'.

Wednesday 28 October

I was woken at 6.30am by the gentle tolling of the bell of St Trophime after a rather restless night, caused by some young Italian students taking a long time to go to bed, but also by too rich fare in the evening. My plan now was to travel by train to Chalon where, in AD 596, queen Brunhilda was on her own with her two restless young grandsons

Theoderic and Theodebert II, trying to rule the whole of Gaul, just at the time when Gregory was sending her most encouraging overtures asking for help for the mission to England. I was almost certain that the town would give some very interesting clues about the Frankish court at that time. I was beginning to wonder about the Rhône and how Augustine could have travelled up it. I was convinced that they had gone by boat up the river to Chalon, but how on earth could they have done that without engines to pull them up, like those long black tug boats I watched as I walked along the footpath. It was food for thought. After a night at Chalon I planned, if possible, to make for Autun and Nevers and then perhaps, my plans were rather vague now, go along the river Loire as I had done once before, long ago, travelling by train from Tours to Lyon. After a good breakfast I was soon in the train, longing to see Provence. It was a delightful experience apart from the speed of the train and the factories that kept blocking the view. I was soon rolling along in real Van Gogh country, his 'Market Garden' and 'The Blue Cart' with hills in blue haze in the far distance, cypresses and vivid autumn trees and forest, cottages and houses with red roofs and bright white fronts, though unfortunately, no view of the Rhône. The train drew in at Avignon and I could see the cathedral in the far distance over the poplars and the jumbled mass of houses and factories. There I had to leave the route of Augustine and his group as they went on steadily upstream in their barge towards Orange. Avignon is famous especially for its medieval bridge. I believe you can even dance 'sous le pont', not *on* but *under* because only four arches remain. The Avignon of the Popes is another matter altogether, and you would need your Baedeker; but by following it all you may begin to lose the thread of your pilgrimage.

Now to Orange where the Romans first met the Cimbri and the Teutons in 105 BC and where a hundred thousand Romans were killed. There is Caesar's most remarkable Triumphal Arch built in 49 BC, and the Roman theatre built in the first century with its statue of the Emperor Augustus, and able to hold seven thousand spectators. There was still no Rhône, but it was lovely to see the orchards and vineyards, and the tree lined road and the ever soft blue mountains. Then ah! The Rhône again at last with its great forest of trees and unkempt woods down to the river's edge, while many of those long black tugboats passed up and down stream. The train now followed the river with fine views of Valence. I, with a sailor's eye, watched the high wind that was blowing upstream, ruffling the water into white waves, and I began to think of how Augustine's bargemaster and his crew would have hauled up the great lug sail. Now the mountains rose on either side and the train stopped at Vienne,

most suitable, because Gregory had prepared commendatory letters for Augustine securing hospitality and assistance from Bishop Desiderius of Vienne and Bishop Aetherius, twenty miles further up the river at the great trading centre of Lyon. Vienne is a city built on the Roman style with its portico, its Forum, a part of which still exists, and the remains of a temple to the goddess Cybele. There are also the remains of a great Roman theatre of the first century AD, capable of holding thirteen thousand spectators. Here, no doubt, Augustine and his group would have paused and have read to them the description of the vicious persecution which took place under Septimiums Severus and described in the epistle of the Gallican Churches of Lyon and Vienne (AD 177).

This epistle carries a long description of the sufferings of faithful Christians young and old. It describes how one young woman, Blandina, was brought into the arena hanging on a stake as food for the wild beasts, but that they would not touch her. She was brought to the gladatorial games daily together with a youth, Ponticus, to watch the punishment of the Christians. Both were pressed

A river cruiser on the Rhône

to forswear their God for idols. They remained constant and the crowd grew furious. They both suffered terribly, never giving up their faith, Ponticus following the zeal of Blandina. He died first, followed soon after by Blandina who died rejoicing and exulting in her death like one invited to a bridal feast rather than one thrown to wild beasts. Even the crowd confessed they had never known any woman to withstand so much suffering and torture.

At Lyon I was turned out of my reserved seat by two old ladies. This great city, one of the largest in France, where the river Rhône rushes down from Lake Geneva to join the river Saône, must have been a place of great importance, for even in 46 BC it was a Roman colony. For the pilgrim who has a day to spare there are in this place, where Augustine and his group stayed and conversed with Bishop Aetherius and were provisioned, some intriguing and inspiring Christian things to see. Apart from all the happy, busy sights and things to do in the city, there is the quite remarkable Musée de la Civilisation Gallo-Romaine à Lyon, recently created by the inspired architect Bernard Zehrfuss, and the arrangement and clarification of the exhibition of Christianity in Gaul is splendid.

The twelfth century cathedral and the nineteenth century basilica on its hill top may be good in their way, but they did not inspire me, with my passion to follow in the footsteps of St Augustine. However, the sixth century church of St Martin d'Ainay rang bells for me for three good reasons. In this church, built on the site of a Roman temple, as Martin and his followers had so often done, Augustine would have been able to share the Eucharist. I once spent a day in medi-

A small quaint figure

tation at this remarkable place. During this time I looked up at the roof to where my eye was taken by a small quaint figure, near the high altar, of a man being immersed in what looked like a well, just like when King Ethelbert was being baptized in the font at St Martin's Canterbury. I was so thrilled to be there as a modern pilgrim because I was meditating in the Lady Chapel where that remarkable and humble priest Paul Couturier used to say Mass. He, perhaps more than anyone else, has helped to inaugurate the movement for unity of all Christians. It was he who was the architect of the Weeks of Prayer for Christian Unity in the 1930s-1940s which have become world wide and gone from strength to strength, on the sound basis of Christians of all denominations being asked to meet together, often in silent prayer to pray 'for the unity of all Christians, as Christ wills and by the means He chooses'. For me that church will always be a special place, for later I went up with Pére Michalon, his disciple, and prayed at Paul Couturier's tomb. Those days in Lyon must have been most heartwarming times. I gather the Weeks of Prayer still play a large part in the churches' ministry there.

I was glad to get once again into the train, leaving, as it were, Augustine and his barge to sail on upstream by the river Saône for Chalon. The scene slowly changed. I could still enjoy the mountains and the woods, but the river was much smaller, there were strong waves with, it seemed, rapids, and I saw a dredger busy at work. Then it began to rain and the whole scene seemed to become drab. As the train drew in at Chalon the city seemed forbidding indeed, full of factories. But I was full of enthusiasm and ready to learn all about queen Brunhilda and her household. Then, after a night or two I planned to go on by train to Autun, Tours, Paris and so to Thanet and Canterbury. But it was not to be. The whole project seemed to fall like a pack of cards around me when I asked the young lady at the ticket office what time the trains went to Tours. I was greatly concerned when she calmly said that the best way to Tours was to go via Paris and so dodge the Loire. After recovering from the initial shock I remembered John Bunyan's lines:

> There's no discouragement
> Shall make him once relent

> His first avowed intent
> To be a pilgrim.

I decided to cut my losses, spend the next day in Chalon and then continue my pilgrimage prosaicly from there to Paris, Boulogne and so go on home. All would not be a complete fiasco for I had now done a large part of the pilgrimage from Rome. From Chalon to Autun, Nevers and down the river Loire to Tours I would have to visualise from the guidebooks. I could still be the pathfinder for the pilgrimage route that Augustine took. I already knew well Tours, Marmoutier, Ligugé and Candes from my previous study of St Martin.

But here I was in Chalon. I used my *Affordable France* to organise my night's lodgings and booked in at an excellent hotel, St George, opposite the station. Its cosy restaurant is known locally for its efficient service and the set menus of outstanding value. I mention it because I was standing in need of encouragement. So, warm and out of the cold, I was able to spend a good time reading up about where Augustine and I had arrived.

Chalon-sur-Saône was a main cross—roads which Julius Caesar chose as a depot for his stores. It became an important centre where the Merovignian king Guntram of the Franks made his centre of government and when he died, passed it over to his nephew Childebert II. When Childebert died in AD 596 the Queen Mother Brunhilda took over and ruled with considerable aplomb. It was she who was ready to welcome Augustine and his companions as they came up the river. Gregory had written to Brunhilda advising her of Augustine's arrival and she had clearly ensured that her young grandsons Theoderic and Theodebert listened carefully to Gregory's latest letter:

> Ever since Almighty God adorned your kingdom with orthodoxy in the faith, and made it remarkable among other nations for its integrity in the Christian religion . . . it has reached us that the English nation, by the mercy of God, desires earnestly to be converted to the Christian faith . . . we have arranged for the despatch of Augustine the servant of God, the bearer of these presents, into those parts . . . we have also instructed them to take with them some presbyters from the neighbourhood, with whose help they may be able to find out what the English mean, and to assist them by their advice, as far as God may permit, in making up their minds . . . and we beseech your Highnesses . . . that our missionaries may obtain your gracious favour. (Mason)

This certainly shows that the Angles were not an ignorant and uncouth people, but that with their king they longed for the blessings of civilisation, codified law and a clear language. Gregory also knew that 'the priests in the neighbourhood who take no notice', were probably the Celtic group which included Columban, who had tried and failed. The English, and Gregory, wanted the more cultured style of St Benedict to guide them.

Thursday 29 October

After a good night in comfortable quarters I set out to explore Chalon. Bishop Gregory of Tours (AD 573–594) describes not only the original cathedral of St Vincent, built around AD 570–580, but also the way of life of the saintly Bishop Agricola who built the church. Augustine and his group would have loudly sung the praises of the cathedral and been there at the Eucharist with Bishop Flavius. It must have been a lovely building. Agricola had been of senatorial family and known for his wisdom and refinement. He was responsible for many building projects including private houses as well as the cathedral, which is adorned with columns, marble and mosaic. Agricola practised extreme abstinence, never eating at midday but only at supper time. He was little versed in the humanities, but he spoke with great eloquence. The original cathedral is heavily overlaid by its neogothic façade and Romanesque nave with many pleasant features, but it does seem as if Bishop Agricolas' columns were the ones that Augustine knew. I felt certain that the Musée Denon, which seemed well appointed, would have much to tell about the Merovingian family with their many raucous ways, but apart from a few sad little artefacts, there was nothing of note. I did find there an excellent excursus by Monsieur Louis Boumanour on how the barges went upstream. The bargees worked with large sweeps to steer the barge close to the bank and the horses or oxen then hauled them along. To see how it was done one only need go to the Victoria and Albert Museum in London and find John Constable's great sketch of the 'Leaping Horse' to see the men working the barge from Flatford to Dedham. Sadly Chalon seemed to have little more to offer, and as my baggage was boring a hole in my shoulder, exhausted I got the next train for Paris. Looking out of the window all looked cold and dull. The white churches, the orchards and the ploughed earth, the charolais cattle, the little rivers here and there a canal and ever the ubiquitous poplars as we sped past Sens and into the sprawling suburbs of Paris.

The Route from Nevers to Canterbury

Friday 30 October

My time in Paris was rather a torment. When I arrived at the Gare du Nord the information bureau was, for me with my deafness, a confusion of noise and bustle. It seemed it would be impossible for me to get to Dunkerque where I had planned I would take the ferry for Ramsgate, coming in by St Augustine's Cross at Ebbsfleet. In the end it was Boulogne that I made for, and the hovercraft dead straight across the Channel to Folkestone, with its parish church of St Mary and St Eanswith on the clifftop to welcome me. I travelled by train to Victoria and arrived home in Somerset safe, sound and thoroughly exhausted. But my pilgrimage was not yet finished.

When Augustine was at Chalon he was very much under the protection of queen Brunhilda, her grandsons and her argumentative courtiers. He also had the full support of the important bishop Syagrius of Autun to whom Gregory had recently given the coveted pallium, the papal gift of a circular band or yoke of lambswool given when a bishop was made a metropolitan. It was considered a great honour and was very important at the court. Syagrius received one of Gregory's letters commendatory encouraging:

> Augustine, a servant of God, of whose earnestness we are confident, along with other servants of God for the good of souls, with the Lord's help, and your Holiness must be forward to help him.

As soon as Augustine and his companions arrived in Autun they would have been aware that they were still under Roman influence for the very name Autun is short for Augustus, and Julius Caesar

Autun

himself felt the area to be 'the sister and rival of Rome itself'. Up in this mountainous area, 750 metres above sea level, excavation has revealed a vast area of 330 acres containing the remains of dwelling houses, a temple and workshops of iron and bronze workers and enamellers. It was the capital of the Aedui and it was Augustus who destroyed it and established his new town called Augustodunum. Augustine and his group had time to see the magnificent two archways, each pierced with four passages, with two high semi-circular arches for wheeled traffic, flanked by two lower ones for pedestrians. There was also a grand Roman theatre which could hold fifteen thousand spectators, a strange temple of Janus, and of course, the magnificent cathedral of Saint Lazare. It would be difficult for us as followers of Augustine's pilgrims not to be captivated by the description of the cathedral, but I quote this description given by bishop Gregory of Tours:

> At this time the church of the blessed martyr Symphorian of Autun was built by the priest Eufronius (AD 555–573) and later on Eufronius was elected as bishop of that city. It was he who, in great devotion,

sent the marble lid which covers the tomb of St Martin. (Gregory of Tours, Book II.15)

It would be exciting if the pilgrim could stop awhile in the cathedral. The first bishop mentioned was Reticius who took part in the Council of Arles, and Martin is never far away.

The Loire

From now on the first pilgrimage route is not so certain, but we know that Gregory sent one of his letters commendatory to Bishop Pelagius of 'Turnis', an unusual spelling for Tours which it must have been as there was no other Gallic see bearing that name, and Pelagius was definitely Bishop of Tours then. Augustine must have been glad to climb down from the mountains to the warmer riverside where he would have stayed as he followed the river Loire from Nevers to Tours. Oscar Wilde wrote of the Loire:

> One of the most wonderful rivers of the world, mirroring from sea to source a hundred cities and five hundred towers.

Although it is now largely unnavigable Arthur and Barbara Eperon in their book *The Loire Valley* wrote:

> The river was the main highway until well into the nineteenth century, the most useful and comfortable way to travel. Roads were awful. Coaches were sprung only with leather straps and horses pulling carts could manage only about five to eight kilometres a days.

Julius Caesar took over control of Nevers, used it as a military depot and granary, stored money and held hostages there and named it Novidunum. In the fifth century the city had its own bishop, and therefore cathedral. The present cathedral is a combination of two buildings and possesses two apses.

The architectural styles are Romanesque and Gothic. Nevers was one of those places that had been forcibly Christianised by the tough old Frankish king Clovis and his charming Christian wife Clotild, who was the great-grandmother of our own English Queen Bertha.

Once Augustine's barge had set off from the quay at Nevers everyone on board would have been able to relax. Pope Gregory in his wisdom had known that the way upstream against the rivers Rhône and Saône was going to take a long time, and so had provided many stops along the way with local bishops ready to give lodgings and provisions. From now on, through this lovely mild country it was only a matter of some 160 kilometres to Tours. With a reasonably powerful current behind them they would have been able to travel between eight and thirteen kilometres an hour, a journey then of some two or three days. They could say their prayers and have their meals without the necessity of anchoring and going ashore. For the modern pilgrim travelling by car, coach or walking there is so much beguiling countryside with beautiful chateaux that it would be easy to lose the thread of following Augustine's pilgrimage. Nowadays the Loire valley draws tourists from all over the world with its wonderful fruit, vegetables

Chateau Neuf sur Loire Musée

and vineyards, towns and the many chateaux. One passes La Charite-sur-Loire; Cosne-sur-Loire with its museum; the heart of Puisaye where St Aunaire had built a hospice to lodge the English on their way to Rome; Briare; Chateauneuf-sur-Loire with its famous chateau and Musée de la Marine de Loire which describes the sad silting up of the river and consequent loss of navigability, Sully with its fourteenth century chateau, and the magnificent Abbey of St Benoit-sur-Loire with its long history, going back to the seventh century and where the relics of St Benedict were brought from Monte Cassino. Then Orleans which even in the third century was a great city which the Romans called Aurelianum, and which was saved from being attacked by Attila the Hun only by the faithful prayer of Bishop St Aignan. In AD 590 it became the principal residence of King Guntram of the Franks, a devotee of Martin of Tours. The modern pilgrim will surely have to visit the massive Cathedral of St Croix built on the site of a tenth century church, some of which is preserved. The

present building was begun in AD 1278 and developed in various different styles, mainly Gothic.

The river then passes by Clery-St-Andre with its fifteenth century church; Beaugency with its church of Notre-Dame and its well known museum; Blois with its great medieval cathedral and chateau; then to Amboise which beckons the modern pilgrim with its famous bridge and its church, where long ago Martin established a monastery. There is also a staggeringly beautiful chateau where Leonardo da Vinci studied. The river flows on and the pilgrim is now in the heart of Martin country. Pope Gregory had arranged Augustine's welcome with Bishop Pelagius of Tours, who had succeeded St Gregory of Tours in AD 594. One can imagine how excited Augustine and his group must have been as their barge tied up at the quay. They must have known straightaway that they were in an almost electric presence, for the whole area was alive with Martin. It was, in fact, called Martinopolis, a city of multitudes of pilgrims thronging around Martin's shrine.

The City of Tours

Tours, the Roman Caesarodonum or Urbs Torones, named after a Gallic tribe, was even then a large city with its own amphitheatre (behind the present cathedral). Around AD 250, as a result of the preaching of St Gatien there grew up a Christian group, and to this day it is possible to visit the caves where the early Christians hid during the persecutions. By AD 371, after the Emperor Constantine had encouraged Christianity, the people of Tours had their own cathedral, but they needed a new bishop. By a trick the citizens took Martin, a retired soldier now living as a hermit near Poitiers, and made him their

Coenbites (monks) of the East (c.4th century) at prayer and basket making

Caves at Marmoutier just outside Tours, where Martin had his hermitage.
St Patrick's cave on extreme left, close to Martin's cell

bishop. In disgust Martin left the bishop's residence and retired to a large meadow by the river at a place called Marmoutier, four kilometres away, where there was a large number of caves in the hillside. Martin built a small hut there to live in and to wait upon God, longing to know God as a man knows a personal friend. Very quickly the whole area became crowded with earnest young men longing also to dedicate themselves to the celibate life for Christ, ready to do whatever He wished. Marmoutier later became one of the greatest intellectual centres of the West with a large abbey which now, sadly, is mostly in ruins. The modern pilgrim should surely go there, for Augus-

tine and his group must have gone there, entering under the fine gateway and making their way past the vegetable plot to find Martin's little hut which by now was made of stone. They would then have climbed the steps to the caves in the hillside where so many dedicated young men kept their silences, and they would have found the one where St Patrick is supposed to have stayed in for some time preparing himself to go to win Ireland for Christ.

At this point Pope Gregory failed to give any further commendatory letters of encouragement to the bishops, apart from the strong supportive letter he sent to the queen Mother Brunhilda's grandsons

Theoderic and Theodebert. Augustine's route to get to Ebbsfleet in Thanet is therefore difficult to follow, and of course the weather began to get much colder. I suggest therefore, that Augustine wintered there at Tours in Martinopolis, and as soon as February was over set out for his journey to England, in 597.

Among the pilgrims foregathering at Martin's shrine would have been many from England who were discovering that the safest routes were the ones where some famous miracle of Martin had been manifested. For example, in AD 589 St Gregory of Tours in his *History of the Franks* wrote this account about our queen Bertha's mother, Queen Ingoberg, who was a devotee of Martin and seemed to have lived quite safely near Le Mans.

> In the fourteenth year of King Childebert's reign there died queen Ingoberg, the widow of Charibert, a woman of great wisdom, devoted to the religious life, constant in her vigils, her prayers and her almsgiving. Warned of her approaching death by God in His providence, or so I believe, she sent messengers to me to ask me to help her to carry out what she wanted to do for the salvation of her soul. She said that she would wait until I arrived and then, when we had talked it over, she would set down in writing what she wanted to be done. I went to her, of course. I found a woman who feared God. She received me most kindly, called a notary and then, after she had discussed her plan with me, as I have told you, left a legacy to Tours cathedral, another to Saint Martin's church and a third to the cathedral at Le Mans. A few months later she was suddenly taken ill and died. By deeds of enfranchisement she freed many serfs. I think that she was in her seventieth year. She left a daughter, who had married the son of a King of Kent. (Gregory of Tours, Book IX.26)

Chartres

Leaving Tours by road or train the next famous place for pilgrims to visit is Chartres. Augustine may also have travelled this way. Martin was much revered in Chartres for it was in this district that he performed one of his most famous miracles. On one of his travels he was walking past a great crowd of heathen when he found a woman wailing because her son had just died. To everyone's surprise Martin brought him back to life again. The crypt of the great cathedral today contains a well that was the focus of ancient druidic ceremonies, and certainly on the evening I attended Eucharist there I felt deeply moved. As Augustine and his group came to the city of the Gallic tribe the Carnutes, they would no doubt have been delighted to see how in AD 596 a new church was being built by the bishop St Bethere, although they had had a bishop and a small cathedral in the fourth century.

The modern pilgrim cannot help but let himself get caught up with the whole story of the way this glorious, yet rather gloomy, great Gothic cathedral with its statues began. It was built over smaller buildings in AD 1195 and 1220 and consecrated in 1260. The pilgrim with time to marvel can look at the splendid glass high up in the windows depicting many of the Gospel stories. The Emperor Constantine is also shown, along with St Martin, King Clovis and his queen Clotild.

After Chartres it seems obvious that all travellers bound from Rome for Canterbury, whichever way they go, will gravitate towards Paris, or as it was called by the Romans, Lutetia. Then it was to them rather insignificant, a busy little town built on an island in the middle of the

Chartres

river Seine where they built a temple to Jupiter which is now the site of the present Cathedral of Notre Dame, on the Ile de la Cité. In AD 508 the Merovingian King Clovis made it his capital and lived there with queen Clotild. In AD 586 Paris was devastated. A woman had prophesied that the whole town would be destroyed by fire, and indeed it was. Houses one after another were set alight, until the fire came to a small oratory built to commemorate how St Martin had once kissed a leper. A man decided that as the flames drew near him he would pin his faith on the miraculous power of Martin. In spite of the wind veering this way and that,

the fire was stayed, and people said that Paris was hallowed from then on. All this devastation must still have been in many people's minds, and the miracle, eleven years later as the pilgrims came in 596–97.

It was King Childebert who in La Cité beside the cathedral of St Etienne built the basilica of Notre Dame which excited the admiration of his contemporaries, and which later in the twelfth century obtained the title of cathedral. It looks as if our modern pilgrim will be able not only to wander around the great Gothic structure with the largest organ in France, 8,500 pipes and 110 stops, but also to go

Notre Dame, Paris

into the remarkable excavations of the foundations of the Merovingian church of St Etienne, where Augustine and his group would almost certainly have kept Eucharist. Nowadays there is High Mass every day at 10am and organ recitals on Sundays between 5.45 and 6.15pm. In Paris there is so much for the pilgrim to love and enjoy from the quiet spirituality of sitting by the river, or chatting in the cafés, to the lighter less spiritual fun to be had. It is such a good place to be in for a while.

The route, then, for all must be by road to Amiens and thence to one of the Channel ports, Boulogne, Calais or Dunkerque, for the river Seine makes a laborious and obscure method of transport. Augustine, fuller more than ever of Martin's miraculous powers and knowing it was wise to travel from Martin site to Martin site for safety, surely must have aimed for Amiens, for it was there that one of the most famous of all the events of Martin's life took place, an occasion that is forever implanted in the mind. As a young under-officer in the Roman army (AD 334) Martin happened to meet a poor man destitute of clothing in the bitter cold as his platoon entered the city gate at Amiens. Martin instinctively divided his cloak in half and gave half to the beggar, amidst the laughter of his soldiers. In the night Martin had a dream, seeing Jesus himself surrounded by a host of angels, and Jesus said to Martin: 'he who is still but a catechumen clothed me with his robe', and Martin hastened to be baptized.

Amiens was the site of the Samarobriva, capital of the tribe of the Ambiani, and in the fourth century Christianity was preached there by St Firmin, its bishop. Its cathedral, however small, was recorded as being in existence in AD 511. Amiens is a thriving city now, having survived the horrors of many wars. The very name of Picardy and the whole area is deeply evocative to those with knowledge of the First World War. Many new development sites in the city have brought to light the vestiges of the Gallo-Roman Amiens that could accomodate fifteen thousand people in its city. Augustine's group would certainly have kept Eucharist there, safely in the footsteps of St Martin. Nowadays the cathedral is an incredible sight, 'a jewel of Gothic art'. Notre Dame of Amiens was built in the thirteenth century and is the largest cathedral, in the world, a classic example of the French Gothic style. It has the well known weeping angel and the astonishing principal organ case built in AD 1549. There are magnificent thirteenth century windows and three thousand six hundred and fifty carved oak figures (AD 1508–1522) in the choir stalls.

CHAPTER SEVEN

Across the Channel to Canterbury

Now the mission was about to come to a head for Augustine. He felt considerable trepidation about meeting the English. Virtually the only way to get to Thanet, where King Ethelbert had told him to await him, was by ship from Boulogne-sur-Mer, the port which the Romans called Gessoriacum, or Itius Portus. It was there in 54 BC that Caesar had mustered some eight hundred ships to invade Britain. The Channel is only about 28 kilometres wide, and from this point Augustine would have been able to see England easily on a clear day, and perhaps even the glint of armour or chariots or people moving. Calais was then but a small fishing village and Dunkerque, though now a thriving and important port, was then almost inaccessible.

St Augustine and his group, leaving behind the sunny memories of Italy, Arles and the Loire had to keep on their warm clothing, and with Amiens behind them, jolt along the way towards Boulogne in wagons or walk across the gloomy countryside. At Boulogne they embarked in a ship to wait for a favourable wind to carry them to Thanet. They would have sailed past Lympne, the Roman Portus Lemanus, and Dover, or Dubris, a very dangerous port, until the cliffs gave way to low hills. Then they would have seen the great fortress of Richborough or Rutupiae where so many thousands of Roman soldiers had been stationed from time to time during the conquest of Britain. The pilot would have steered the ship through the tricky waters navigating carefully to the small harbour at Ebbsfleet, on the island of Thanet and there they landed. The Venerable Bede described it thus:

On the east of Kent is the large Isle of Thanet containing according to the English way of reckoning, 600 families, divided from the other land by the river Wantsum, which is about three furlongs over, and fordable only in two places, for both ends of it run into the sea. In this island landed the servant of our Lord, Augustine, and his companions, being, as is reported, nearly forty men. They had, by order of the blessed Pope Gregory, taken interpreters of the nation of the Franks, and sending to Ethelbert, signified that they were come from Rome, and brought a joyful message, which most undoubtedly assured to all that took advantage of it everlasting joys in heaven, and a kingdom that would never end, with the living and true God. The king having heard this, ordered them to stay in that island where they had landed, and that they should be furnished with all necessaries, till he should consider what to do with them. For he had before heard of the Christian religion, having a Christian wife of the royal family of the

Franks, called Bertha; whom he had received from her parents, upon condition that she should be permitted to practise her religion with the Bishop Liudhard, who was sent with her to preserve her faith. Some days after, the king came to the island, and sitting in the open air, ordered Augustine and his companions to be brought into his presence. For he had taken precaution that they should not come to him in any house, lest, according to an ancient superstition, if they practised any magical arts, they might impose upon him, and so get the better of him. (Bede, Book I.25)

I must here confess that if my pilgrimage has been a bit cursory up until now I have been but spying out the land, pathfinding, for fellow pilgrims who I hope will have more leisure to savour the many places of pilgrimage. But now I was home in Thanet and I know the area so thoroughly well, the footpaths and lanes and my dear river Great Stour. I lived on the Isle of Thanet for eight years as vicar of Birchington, before moving to St Martin's church in Canterbury with all the joy of celebrating the Eucharist week by week, and imagining Augustine doing the same with queen Bertha there.

I have drawn a map to show what Thanet must have looked like when Augustine arrived in April or May of 597 at Ebbsfleet, where the Saxons called 'the stream where the hips grow'. As to his route to Canterbury I have largely followed the classic account of the 'Landing of Augustine' given by Dean Arthur Stanley in his *Historical Memorials of Canterbury* and the excellent books produced on St Martin's church by Canon C. Routledge which I feel cannot be bettered. I have read all that I could find from the learned journals of 1897 that led to a spate of discussion in that centenary

year, and also any discussions I could find since, but I am more than ever convinced that Arthur Stanley was right about Ebbsfleet, and that the St Augustine's stone cross, erected among the lavender beds by the 2nd Earl Granville in 1884 to commemorate the landing by Augustine in England was well on the right lines, and marked Augustine's camp. It is good to know that the Canterbury Archaeological Trust and the Thanet Trust for Archaeology are continuing to excavate sites in the area, which whets the appetite for more news.

Thanet, as Augustine soon found, is a charming island approximately 11 or 12 kilometres from east to west, and 6 to 8 kilometres from north to south with rich loam and brown earth which makes it some of the best soil in Britain. The Wantsum estuary at its closest to the mainland in those days was some 550 metres wide and thus made a safe passage for ships bound for London to avoid the dangerous seas and cliffs of the North Foreland, although even then the Wantsum was very slowly beginning to silt up with sand and mud. One of the monks long ago wrote:

> Well rounded island, Thanet, which encircles the waves, fertile and elegant, second to none in the world.

Because of its many bright beacons the Romans had called it Taneta or Rum, and loved it. But after they left it was the savage Jutes from Denmark who in AD 450 took it over with their long ships, led by Kings Hengist and Horsa. It was from them that King Ethelbert was descended. To this day it is quite an adventure for the modern pilgrim, after seeing St Augustine's Cross to go the extra kilometre or so to the seaside to see the viking ship, the 'Hugin'

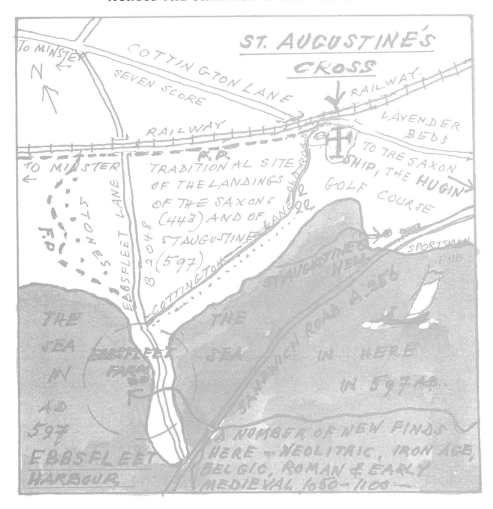

Thanet when Augustine arrived in AD597

which fifty three valiant Danes rowed across the North Sea in 1948 to mark the centenary of the arrival of the Saxons.

King Ethelbert had given firm instructions that he would provide 'all the necessaries' for Augustine and his group, and that they were definitely to stay in open ground and not settle near a city, town or village. So after landing on the quay at Ebbsfleet I can visualise the group walking with their baggage and horses provided by Ethelbert along the old road, Cottington Lane, to St Augustine's Cross to where a large shed or tent must have

been set up and a good well dug. This well can still be seen next to the 'Sportsman' inn near the golf course. Thanet in April or May can be very cold, so the fire would have been kept blazing by them, though this same wind blowing from either north east or south east makes sailing up the Stour easy, as I know from having done it.

Let the Venerable Bede take up his narrative:

Some days after, the King came into the island, and sitting in the open air, ordered

'They came . . . bearing a silver cross'

Augustine and his companions to be brought into his presence . . . They came furnished with Divine, not with magical virtue, bearing a silver cross for their banner, and the image of our Lord and Saviour painted on a board; and singing the litany, they offered up their prayers to the Lord for the eternal salvation both of themselves and of those to whom they were come. When he had sat down, pursuant to the King's commands, and preached to them and his attendants there present, the word of life, the king answered thus: 'Your words and promises are very fair, but as they are new to us, and of uncertain import, I cannot approve of them so far as to forsake that which I have so long followed with the whole English nation. But because you are come from far into my kingdom, and, as I conceive, are desirous to impart to us those things which you believe to be true, and most beneficial, we will not molest you, but give you favour-

able entertainment, and take care to supply you with your necessary sustenance; nor do we forbid you to preach and gain as many as you can to your religion'. Accordingly he permitted them to reside in the city of Canterbury, which was the metropolis of all his dominions, and pursuant to his promise, besides allowing them sustenance, did not refuse them liberty to preach'. (Bede, Book I.25)

The doors of England were now open for the missionaries, so they could make their way to Canterbury, where King Ethelbert and queen Bertha with bishop Liudhard had their residence. Queen Bertha and bishop Liudhard had for a long time been praying for the conversion of the English nation in the little church of St Martin on the hillside which was built over the ruins of an older Romano-British church. Here Ethelbert had prepared for them a dwelling place so they could live for a while in the city to see if the English people would accept the Christian faith. The site of their residence is called Stable Gate and is situated by the old church of St Alphege, near to the cathedral, and now houses a museum and publicity centre for the city.

No one will ever know precisely which way Augustine travelled to Canterbury, but there is a longstanding tradition that the group landed in Richborough from Thanet, having sailed over from Ebbsfleet. The modern pilgrim might like to know how the centenary of 1897 took place. I found a description of it in the *Kentish Gazette* of July 1897. The Lambeth Conference was sitting at the time so the whole one hundred Archbishops and Bishops, after a service in St Martin's

church travelled by train from Canterbury West station to a temporary platform which had been erected for them at the railway arch near Minster, by the lavender fields. The Primate in his robes climbed down out of his coach, but some unfortunate porter had forgotten to bring the key to let the bishops come out of their carriages, and this caused considerable fuss. However, at last they all climbed out, including the cathedral choir preceded by the silver cross, and sang 'Onward Christian Soldiers'. A vast crowd had gathered and prayers were said by St Augustine's Cross. Once again on board the train the official party made for Sandwich, and then by carriage to Richborough where they went to look at the Romano-Saxon chapel, for St Augustine is supposed to have landed on English soil here. An excellent tea was laid on in a large marquee. Not to be outdone, the bishops, clergy and laity of the Roman Catholic community did the same thing later. Let the modern pilgrim follow suit by going to Sandwich by bus, car, coach or train (Minster station) and make their way to Richborough, so important to the beginnings of Christianity here, which it is fairly easy to trace with the excellent guide books and the museum full of artefacts found there, and maintained by English Heritage.

Modern pilgrims longing for journey's end at St Martin's church and the cathedral in Canterbury will, like Augustine, use one of three routes to foregather near St Martin's. The first is the easiest but rather prosaic, passing as it does along the lane from Richborough to the main A257, one of the old Roman roads. Walking through pleasant countryside and villages such as Ash, Wingham and Littlebourne, they will come to the bottom of

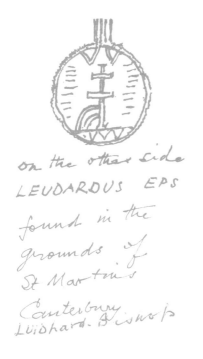

on the other side
LEUDARDUS EPS
found in the
grounds of
St Martin's
Canterbury
Luidhard. Bishop

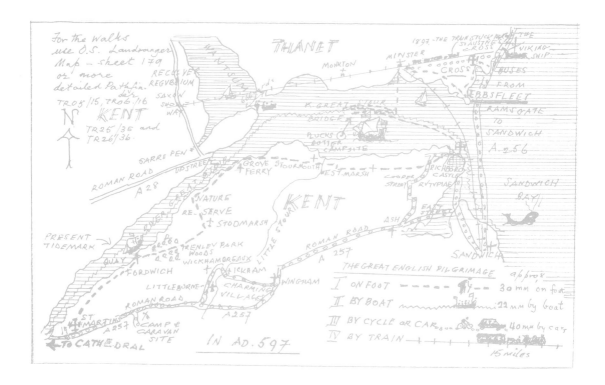

the hill into Canterbury where there is a right turning to the bottom of St Martin's hill, and so to St Martin's church.

Another way is more energetic and can be done in a day. I discovered this when I was following the Stour Valley footpaths and realised I was walking right over Augustine country. Leaving Richborough Castle by the west gate and walking over the cobbles, where so many Roman legionary feet must have also trod, I discovered that the footpath before me followed the line of the old Roman road to Grove Ferry and then to Reculver (Rutupiae) one way and Canterbury the other. In my book *Six Walks along the River Stour* I describe all this in some detail with black and white illustrations. A similar walk starts from the amphitheatre in Richborough and is described in a book produced by Kent County Council, called *The Stour Valley Walk* of which I wrote

the part that involves the walks from Canterbury to Sandwich. It is fascinating countryside full of interest; Westmarsh, East Stourmouth and Stodmarsh with its famous nature reserve. Then there is the little town of Fordwich at the tidal limit of the river with its Tudor court house, and finally the breathtaking first sight looking down, of the city of Canterbury.

One can then slip along the footpath to St Martin's church.

Finally, there is the third rather sedate way of doing the journey on a sunny day! Augustine and the senior members with their baggage, I am sure, embarked at Richborough quay, and sailed up to Fordwich harbour with the tide. That adventure nowadays, however, needs a boatman from Sandwich or Grove Ferry.

Arriving at the top of Garrison Hill or the top of the churchyard on St Martin's Hill we can look down on the city below. Dean Stanley wrote:

> Let anyone sit on the hill of the little church of St Martin, and look on the view which is there spread before his eyes . . . the view is indeed one of the most inspiriting that can be found in the world.

Augustine may well have stood here too and gazed at the city of Canterbury below with the smoke rising from the chimneys of the rough houses. The Venerable Bede wrote of Augustine's arrival:

> It is reported that, as they drew near to the city, after their manner, with the holy cross, and the image of our sovereign Lord and King, Jesus Christ, they, in concert sung this litany: 'We beseech thee, O Lord, in all thy mercy, may thy anger and wrath be turned away from this city, and from thy holy house, because we have sinned. Halleujah'. As soon as they entered the dwelling place assigned them, they began to imitate the course of life practised in the primitive church; applying themselves to frequent prayer, watching and fasting; preaching the word of life to as many as they could; despising all worldly things, as not belonging to them; receiving only their necessary food from those they taught; living themselves in all respects in conformity with the others, and being always disposed to suffer any adversity

After G. Shepherd, St Augustine's Gate, Canterbury

and even to die for that truth which they preached. In short, several believed and were baptized, admiring the simplicity of their innocent life, and the sweetness of their heavenly doctrine. There was on the east side of the city, a church dedicated to the honour of St Martin built whilst the Romans were still in the island, wherein the queen, who, as has been said before was a Christian, used to pray. In this they first began to meet, to sing, to pray, to say mass, to preach and to baptize, till the king, being converted to the faith, allowed them to preach openly, and build or repair churches in all places. (Bede, Book I.25,26)

Now at journey's end the modern pilgrim can see the ruins of the abbey of Augustine where Christian learning and culture first took root in Britain. There also is the great cathedral. It is perhaps time to recollect how Augustine's mission to bring Christianity to these shores gave rise to so many brilliant cultural ideas, and even our English language itself, which has now become almost universally under-stood. Our great Church of England tradi-tion entwined with the monarchy all stems from this first great mission. Our willingness to express new kinds of Christian unity and so much more must surely stem from St Gregory's first vision of a mission to England at St Andrew's monastery on the Caelian Hill in Rome.

So at last the pilgrim comes down to the church of St Martin's. At first it seems just like any other ordinary parish church, but to those who pick up the guide book it will quickly become clear that all the stones of the church are mixed regularly with the red tiles and plaster that the pilgrim has found so often on his travels from Rome to Richborough; in short he is in a place where the early Christians of the fourth and fifth centu-ries worshipped. One senses this is a deeply holy place. As a pilgrim, kneel or sit quietly for some twenty minutes, as I have done so often, and aided by Martin's powerful influence, say little Samuel's uncomprehending words to God:
'Speak Lord, for I am listening.' (1 Sam. 3.10) Look at the font which used to stand in the middle of the nave. There has been a long tradition that it was here

at the time of Ethelbert's baptism, and certainly in the sixth and seventh cen-turies this style of font was well known. Bede describes how:

> When King Ethelbert, among the rest, in-duced by the unspotted life of these holy men, and their delightful promises, which, by many miracles, they proved to be most certain, believed and was baptized, greater numbers began daily to flock together to hear the word, and, forsaking their hea-then rites, to associate themselves, by be-lieving, to the unity of the church of Christ. Their conversion the king so far encouraged, as that he compelled none to embrace Christianity, but only showed more affection to the believers, as to his fellow citizens in the heavenly kingdom. (Bede, Book I.26)

Gregory wrote to Ethelbert when he heard of his conversion expressing his great joy, congratulating him on becom-ing a very new Emporer Constantine.

The pilgrim has not quite finished his or her pilgrimage. Leaving the little church of St Martin, walk down the old Roman road, now the A257, past the grounds of St Augustine's Abbey to Lady Wootton's Green. Cross the main road and pass through the city wall by the little Queningate which is known to have been used by Bertha as she walked to St Martin's. Augustine would also have known this route well. Enter the cathedral which is so magnificent, and recall Bede's descrip-tion of the cathedral which stood there, and which Augustine would have known:

> An episcopal see had been given to Augus-tine in the king's own city, he regained possession, with the king's support, of a church there which he was informed had been built in the city long before by the Roman believers. (Bede, Book I.33)

A warm welcome can be expected from

St Boniface baptizing a king.
(Martyred in AD 754)

the clergy and cathedral staff. I would suggest that pilgrims make straight for the chapel of Our Lady of the Undercroft, one of those holy, quiet places that has a sense of awe all of its own, and ask for a blessing of thanksgiving and prayer for the unity of all Christians. There pilgrims may light a candle for their family, church, the leaders of people, and for the conversion of all unbelievers. Then they may go on their way cherishing the card of blessing.

Let the penultimate words of our pilgrimage come from Ireland, in that little book called *Columbanus, in his own Words* by Tomas O Fiaich when he wrote:

I have returned to Bobbio many times since my first visit. Perhaps the most interesting time was in 1978 when I accompanied a BBC Northern Ireland camera team in the footsteps of St Columban from the English Channel to his tomb at Bobbio. They were a mixed group of Protestants and Catholics, Unionists and Nationalists, and the director of the film was a Presbyterian clergyman. I noticed then how we all looked back to Columban as a father-figure whom we shared. It is no wonder the film was later awarded an Italian prize.

But let the final word, a blessing, come from that cynosure of all pilgrims, John Bunyan, in his *The Pilgrim's Progress* which he wrote, cooped up in his prison cell:

I see myself at the end of my journey, my toilsome days are ended. I am going now to see that head that was crowned with thorns, and that face that was spit upon for me. I have formerly lived by hearsay and faith; but now I go where I shall live by sight, and shall be with him in whose company, I delight myself. I have loved to hear my Lord spoken of; and wherever I have seen the print of his shoe in the earth, there I have coveted to set my foot too.

The St Augustine's seat, Canterbury Cathedral

Notes and Prayers for Pilgrims

We are not strangers but Ecumenical Pilgrims

Before setting out on pilgrimage it is recommended that pilgrims begin by asking for a blessing from their parish priest or minister at the Holy Communion, or Eucharist. They may like to bring with them a shell and, possibly, a small icon or picture (to prop up in their lodgings) which shows, perhaps, how the three angels appeared to Abraham at Mamre (Genesis 18.1–15) by Andrei Rublev, Moscow.

> 'It was by faith that Abraham obeyed the call to set out for a country that was the inheritance given to him and his descendants, and THAT HE SET OUT WITHOUT KNOWING WHERE HE WAS GOING' (Hebrews 1.8)

Bunyan's Theme Song

John Bunyan, the tinker of Bedford, was born in 1628 and died in 1688. He was a Puritan, or extreme English Protestant. Because of his insistence on preaching openly he was cast into a dungeon at Bedford by the Cavaliers and clergy of the day. He was left there for twelve years, and was once even threatened with the 'stretch'. Whilst there, in absolute destitution, he wrote the book *The Pilgrim's Progress*; this song by John Bunyan, is usually set to the tune Monks Gate, adapted from an English traditional melody by R. Vaughen Williams (1872–1958).

> Who would true valour see,
>   let him come hither;
> one here will constant be,
>   come wind, come weather;
> there's no discouragement
> shall make him once relent
> his first avowed intent
>   to be a pilgrim.
>
> Whoso beset him round
>   with dismal stories,
> do but themselves confound;
>   his strength the more is.
> No lion can him fright;
>   he'll with a giant fight,
> but he will have the right
>   to be a pilgrim.
>
> No goblin nor foul fiend
>   can daunt his spirit;
> he knows he at the end
>   shall life inherit.
> Then, fancies, fly away;
> he'll not fear what men say;
> he'll labour night and day
>   to be a pilgrim.

A Pilgrim's special Meditation or Mantra

A mantra may be used repeatedly in the silences or when sleepless in the night.

This first mantra is from I Samuel 3.2–14: the boy Samuel in his linen loincloth was serving in the temple. The lamp was not gone out when he heard a voice saying 'Samuel, Samuel'. He ran to the old priest Eli and said, 'Here I am, you called me'. Eli said, 'I did not call, go back and lie down'. This happened three times, until in the end Eli realised it was the Lord calling him, so he said, 'Next time if someone calls, say:

SPEAK LORD, YOUR SERVANT IS LISTENING'.

When Samuel did he had much to hear from the Lord. All Christians in the end of their silences hear clearly from God messages in the secret movings in their minds, often like hunches.

A second mantra is a comfortable Aramaic word, that burst from St Paul's first letter to the Corinthians (ch 16.22) in his own hand

MARANATHA (our Lord comes)

A third mantra is the word that Francis of Assisi, full of joy or ecstasy, kept crying one whole night until the dawn

MY GOD! MY GOD!

The Liturgy or Public Services of the Churches

These services emerged from the life of the early Christian gatherings in the third or fourth generation, some seventeen hundred or more years ago. It was St Benedict (480–550) who clarified the daily round of services that we still use in a large number of the churches in the West. Here we are exploring our own very spiritual roots, as in our pilgrimage we enter so many chapels, parish churches, cathedrals and monasteries, and can feel ourselves at home in the whole Household of God.

The reading for the suggested services could be those provided by the current Week of Prayer for Christian Unity (published by the Council of Churches for Britain and Ireland, Inter-Church House, 35–41 Lower Marsh London SE1 7RL)

The services used could include the familiar Gregorian chant for the Veni-Creator which Gregory himself could have fathered; certainly it is the only song used in the old Book of Common Prayer.

Evenings could end with the beautiful service of COMPLINE using the Gregorian chant Te Lucis, so familiar to many. If the Latin words are used it will not be difficult to identify with Augustine and his companions on their pilgrimage.

Te lucis ante terminum	Procul recedant somnia,
Rerum Creator, poscimus,	Et noctium phantasmata;
Ut pro tua clementia	Hostemque nostrum comprime,
Sis Praesul et custodia.	Ne polluantur corpora.

Praesta, Pater piissime,
Patrique compar Unice,
Cum Spiritu Paraclito
Regnans per omne saeculum. Amen.

The Ecumenical Pilgrimage

The pilgrimage is not just a holiday (or excursion). It is a serious call to explore our own spiritual roots and to trace how the Holy Spirit is working here and now for the restoration of unity among all Christians. This Godly exercise, however, will also bring in its train some of the most exciting cultural, architectural, artistic and panoramic views in the world.

Pilgrims will thrill as they come to terms with the origin of the Ecumenical Movement, which spontaneously sprang up in the 1950s and 1960s in the West, and found a great impetus when Pope John XXIII on Christmas Day 1961 convoked the Vatican II Council. He invited all representatives of Christians separated from the Roman Catholic church to be present as observers. To them all in his apostolic constitution he wrote:

'Renew your wonders (Lord), in our time, as though for a new Pentecost.

Ecumenism means in Greek a house, or household: we are the Household of God.

In the pilgrimage described in this book we can sense ecumenism in many ways in Rome itself, and other places on the way, but when we come to Lyon it becomes palpable as we pray, for instance, at St Martin's where the Abbé Coutourier often celebrated Mass. The Abbé Coutourier was a very humble schoolmaster of a religious order in the 1950s, yet there came to him one of those dynamic visions that come out of religious devotion and deep silences, and change the world. In days gone by, prayers used to be made by Christians being achieved by individual conversions of those not of their own faith; however the Abbé realised that Jesus in St John's gospel said:

I PRAY NOT ONLY FOR THESE (his own disciples) BUT FOR THOSE ALSO WHO THROUGH THEIR WORDS WILL BELIEVE IN ME. MAY THEY ALL BE ONE, FATHER, MAY THEY BE ONE IN US AS YOU ARE IN ME AND I AM IN YOU, SO THAT THE WORLD MAY BELIEVE IT WAS YOU WHO SENT ME.

Out of Coutourier's endless letters to the spiritual leaders of the world sprang the Weeks of Prayer for Christion Unity in Lyon. The idea caught on like fire and now the week of Prayer throughout the world, either the week 18–25 January or during the Ascensiontide/Pentecost season, is prepared by a group from a different continent each year. Often too, Christians throughout the world light a candle on the Thursdays of their lives to remember Jesus' priestly prayer for the unity of all Christians, and sit quietly for half an hour.

When the pilgrims arrive at Mâcon or Chalon-sur-Saône it is almost impossible that they will not be led, as it were by strings of love, to a most exciting diversion to see the kind of way that the Ecumenical Vision of the future is being clothed. As Pope John XXIII once cried, 'Ah! Taizé, that little springtime'.

In 1942 the village of Taizé, in France, had a neglected parish church. Under the charismatic leadership of a Protestant pastor, Roger Schutz-Marranche, a group of young men (so familiar now in their simple white robes) joined him and dedicated themselves to Godly silences and a new kind of chanting that fascinates many, especially young people under thirty.

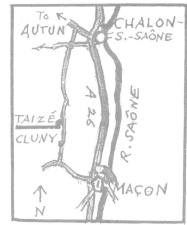

They were determined to let the ecumenical vision take over, at any rate in their own community, in an open-ended dialogue with all who come. In the early days the Abbé Coutourier stayed with them and celebrated Mass in the deserted church. Now the community with the blessing of the Pope has Roman Catholic and Anglican brothers in the community, and has the encouragment of Eastern Orthodox members too.

With the many brothers now working throughout the world they never take money, but always do their own work, and encourage all to come, with their great tents and meetings that go on from year to year. Every pilgrim should surely warm to their vision and if possible experience their enthusiasm, by a visit or by reading *The Story of Taizé* by J. L. Gonzalez Balado (Mowbray/Cassell).

Finally, no pilgrims will be worth their salt unless they have had a sense of sorrow for their own lives and for the mess we are making of our world. So as they leave St Martin's hill in Canterbury let someone take out a copy of that treasure the Book of Common Prayer, that Archbishop Cranmer collated from the ancient fathers of the Church, and lead them down the LONGPORT past the prison, saying or singing the LITANY and carrying their cross and Bible, just as Augustine and the forty companions did, into the cathedral, and as I used to with the children's Litany on Good Friday.

In the cathedral as the pilgrims make their way down into the chapel of Our Lady of the Undercroft asking for the prayers and blessing from the priest, they should then light a candle and pray in silence for their own homes and families and for the whole HOUSEHOLD OF GOD. Some, too, may love to use the beautiful ecumenical devotion giving thanks for the life and example of the Blessed Virgin Mary.

1. V. The angel of the Lord announced unto Mary.
   R. And she conceived by the Holy Spirit.
   Hail Mary, full of grace, the Lord is with thee, blessed art thou among women and blessed is the fruit of thy womb, Jesus. (Luke 1.26–38)

2. V. Behold the handmaid of the Lord.
   R. Be it unto me according to thy word.
   Hail Mary, full of grace, the Lord is with thee, blessed art thou among women and blessed is the fruit of thy womb, Jesus.

3. V. The Word was made flesh.
   R. And dwelt among us. (John 1.14)
   Hail Mary, full of grace, the Lord is with thee, blessed art thou among women and blessed is the fruit of thy womb, Jesus.

A PRAYER

We beseech thee, O Lord, pour thy grace into our hearts; that as we have known the Incarnation of thy Son Jesus Christ by the message of an angel, so by his cross and Passion we may be brought into the glory of his Resurrection; through the same Jesus Christ our Lord. Amen.

Further Hymn Prayers

Come, Holy Ghost, our souls inspire,
And lighten with celestial fire;
Thou the anointing Spirit art,
Who dost thy sevenfold gifts impart:

Thy blessed unction from above
Is comfort, life, and fire of love;
Enable with perpetual light
The dullness of our blinded sight:

Anoint and cheer our soilèd face
With the abundance of thy grace:
Keep far our foes, give peace at home;
Where thou art guide no ill can come.

Teach us to know the Father, Son,
And thee, of Both, to be but One;
That through the ages all along
This may be our endless song,

Praise to thy eternal merit,
Father, Son, and Holy Spirit. Amen.

JOHN COSIN (1594–1672)
based on *Veni creator Spiritus*

Guide me, O thou great Redeemer,
pilgrim through this barren land;
I am weak, but thou art mighty;
hold me with thy powerful hand:
bread of heaven,
feed me now and evermore.

Open now the crystal fountain
whence the healing stream doth flow;
let the fiery cloudy pillar
lead me all my journey through:
strong deliverer,
be thou still my strength and shield.

When I tread the verge of Jordan,
bid my anxious fears subside;
death of death, and hell's destruction,
land me safe on Canaan's side:
songs and praises
I will ever give to thee.

W. WILLIAMS (1717–91)
Welsh, tr. P. and W. WILLIAMS

1. O happy band of pilgrims,
   if onward ye will tread
with Jesus as your fellow
   to Jesus as your Head.

2. O happy if ye labour
   as Jesus did for men;
O happy if ye hunger
   as Jesus hungered then.

3. The cross that Jesus carried
   he carried as your due:
the crown that Jesus weareth
   he weareth it for you.

4. The faith by which ye see him,
   the hope in which ye yearn,
the love that through all troubles
   to him alone will turn,

5. the trials that beset you,
   the sorrows ye endure,
the manifold temptations
   that death alone can cure,

6. what are they but his jewels
   of right celestial worth?
what are they but the ladder
   set up to heaven on earth?

7. O happy band of pilgrims,
   look upward to the skies,
where such a light affliction
   shall win so great a prize.

J. M. NEALE (1818–66)

St Martin's font, Canterbury

Bibliography

Bautier Robert-Henri, *The Economic Development of Medieval Europe*. Thames and Hudson. 1971

Bede. The Venerable, *Ecclesiastical History of the English People*. Giles, J.A., George Bell & Sons. 1894

Bright, William. DD, *Early English Church History*. (3rd Edition). Oxford. 1897

Cutts, Edward L. DD, *Augustine of Canterbury*. Methuen & Co. 1895

Donaldson, Christopher, *Martin of Tours, Parish Priest, Mystic and Exorcist*. Routledge and Kegan Paul. 1980

Eliot, T.S., *Four Quartets*. Faber

Gregory of Tours, *The History of the Franks*. Lewis Thorpe, Ph.D. Penguin Classics. 1974

Lecoy de la Marche, A, *St Martin*. Alfred Mame et fils. 1881

Lightfoot, J.B., *S. Clement of Rome. The Two Epistles to the Corinthians*. Macmillan & Co. 1869

Ed. Mason, Arthur J. DD, *The Mission of St Augustine to England according to the Original Documents* being a Handbook for the Thirteenth Centenary. Cambridge. 1897

O Fiaich, Tomas, *Columbanus in his own Words*. Veritas, Dublin. 1974

Pautier, R-H., *The Economic Development of Medieval Europe*. Thames & Hudson. 1971

Plummer, C. MA, *Baedae Opera Historica* Tomes I and II. Oxford. 1896

Richards, Jeffrey, *The Consul of God* The Life and Times of Gregory the Great. Routledge and Kegan Paul. 1980

Routledge, C.F. MA, FSA, *The History of St Martin's Church Canterbury*. Kegan Paul, Trench, Trubner & Co. Ltd. 1891

Routledge, C.F. MA FSA, *The Church of St Martin Canterbury*. George Bell & Sons. 1901

Stanley, Arthur, *Historical Memorials of Canterbury* Everymans Library. J.M. Dent. 1906

Tacitus (Grant), *Tacitus on Imperial Rome*. Penguin Classics

—*Archaeologia Cantiana* being the transactions of Kent Archaeological Society

—*Encyclopaedia Britannica* (11th Edition). 1910

—*The Epistles of St Gregory the Great*

Guidebooks
—*Affordable France*
—*Affordable Italy*
—Fodor's Travel Publications Inc. 1992

Donaldson, Christopher, *Six Walks along the Stour* (from Canterbury to Ebbsfleet). Meresborough Books. 1985

—*Stour Valley Walks*. Stour Valley Society. 1974, 1979, 1982

Eperon, A and B, *The Loire Valley*. Christopher Helm

Masson, G., *The Companion Guide to Rome*. Harper Collins (6th Ed). 1957

Morton, H.V., *A Traveller in Rome*. Methuen & Co Ltd. 1957

Rossiter, S. MA, *The Blue Guides. Rome and environs*. Ernest Benn Ltd. 1971

Index

(Principal characters in **bold face**. Illustrations in *Italic figures*)